FINANCIAL
RISK MANAGEMENT
FUNDAMENTALS

JASON SCHENKER

FINANCIAL RISK MANAGEMENT FUNDAMENTALS

BY JASON SCHENKER

ISBN: 978-1-946197-25-2 *Paperback*
      978-1-946197-19-1 *Ebook*

PRESTIGE
PROFESSIONAL PUBLISHING

For my fellow risk professionals.

CONTENTS

CONTENTS

CONTENTS

RISK MANAGEMENT

Risk management has been a big part of my professional career.

It was a part of my graduate degree in applied economics, and it has been a part of every professional role I held thereafter.

In my first job out of grad school, I joined Wachovia Bank, which was the third-largest bank in the United States at the time. I became the Chief Energy Economist and held other functional titles and roles in which risk management was critical. I worked with clients exposed to currency, commodity, and interest rate risks. And I served on several different risk committees within the bank.

Just ahead of the financial crisis, I left banking and joined McKinsey & Company as a Risk Specialist in the risk practice, where I worked with clients to build hedging, risk management, and trading strategies. And I also provided content direction to teams on six continents about currency, commodity, interest rates, and other risks.

Ever since I left McKinsey to found Prestige Economics in 2009, I have continued to advise corporate clients, industry groups, institutional investors, and corporate boards about currency, commodity, and interest rate risks.

And in this book, I get to share my knowledge and experience of risk management with you.

The main goal of *Financial Risk Management Fundamentals* is to introduce you to the importance of risk management fundamentals and core principles, as well as to prepare you to support risk management projects and initiatives. This book has been carefully crafted to provide digestible explanations of complex concepts. To meet these goals, I have structured a mix of explanations, anecdotes, and graphics to provide context and relevance to what can be an otherwise esoteric finance topic.

Acknowledgements

I want to acknowledge and thank all of the people who were involved in one way or another with the process of making this book come together. And there are some specific individuals I need to thank.

First, I want to thank **Nawfal Patel** and my other colleagues at Prestige Economics, as well as everyone at Prestige Professional Publishing who helped me bring this book to fruition.

Additionally, I need to thank the wonderful and talented people at **LinkedIn Learning**, including Jolie Miller, Megan Russell, Dianne Starke, and many others!

This book was created as a companion to a course I recorded in 2017 titled *Finance Foundations: Risk Management*. If you like this book, you will really enjoy the online course. Plus, the course should be eligible for continuing education hours in 2019!

You can find my LinkedIn Learning course online: https://www.linkedin.com/learning/finance-foundations-risk-management

Finally, and most importantly, I want to thank my family for supporting me as I worked on this book. I dedicated this book to my fellow risk professionals, but I am always most grateful for the support of my loving wife, **Ashley Schenker**, and to both of my parents — my father, **Jeffrey Schenker**, as well as my mother, **Janet Schenker**.

My family has supported me in countless ways over the years by providing emotional support and editorial feedback.

Every time I write a book, it's a crazy experience that spills over into my family life, so to them and to everyone else who helped me in this process, thank you!

Finally, thank you for buying this book.

I hope you enjoy *Financial Risk Management Fundamentals*!

~ Jason Schenker

THE IMPORTANCE OF FINANCIAL RISK MANAGEMENT FUNDAMENTALS

Risk management isn't something most companies think about until it's too late. Wouldn't you like to be the one who thinks about things before they go bad?

Imagine if you could have saved Enron from imploding or Blockbuster from being wiped away — or if you could have prevented the financial crisis of 2008. Making risk management a priority could have prevented all of these things.

It's too late to change the past, but as an ancient Chinese proverb says, the best time to plant a tree was 20 years ago. The second-best time is now.

This is why I structured this book to cover the critical basics and fundamentals of financial risk management, to get you ready to help protect your company or business from financial and non-financial risks.

In order to tackle the most important financial risk management fundamentals, I have divided this book into seven sections:

- **Purpose and Process of Risk Management**
- **Four Non-Financial Risks**
- **Five Financial Risks**
- **Financial Risk Overview**
- **Risk Management Solutions**
- **Corporate Risk Management**
- **Pulling Everything Together**

In the first section of the book, **Purpose and Process of Risk Management**, I provide a framework for considering the importance of risk in corporations in Chapter 2. I also discuss the risk management process in Chapter 3 and the importance of following a process in Chapter 4. I also discuss why I wrote this book in Chapter 1.

In the second section, **Four Non-Financial Risks**, I discuss four non-financial risks. In Chapter 5, I discuss operational risk, and in Chapter 6, I discuss strategic risk. Thereafter, in Chapter 7, I discuss reputation risk. Then, as the fourth non-financial risk, I discuss regulatory risk in Chapter 8.

The third section of the book includes my discussion of the different **Five Financial Risks**. This meaty part of the book includes a discussion of business risk in Chapter 9 and market risk in Chapter 10. Then, in Chapters 11, 12, and 13, I discuss credit risk, liquidity risk, and counterparty risk, respectively.

In the fourth section of the book, I discuss a **Financial Risk Overview**. This includes a discussion of interest rate, foreign exchange, and commodity market risks in Chapter 14. In Chapter 15, I discuss direct and indirect risks.

In the fifth section, **Risk Management Solutions**, I discuss financial risk management solutions broadly in Chapter 16, before discussing specific financial risk management solutions. In Chapter 17, I discuss put and call options. In Chapter 18, I discuss interest rate swaps. In Chapter 19, I discuss futures and forward agreements. Then, in Chapters 20 and 21, I discuss some financial risk management solution cost drivers, including the impact standardization and time, as well as liquidity and volatility. I further discuss non-financial solutions in Chapter 22.

In the sixth section of the book, **Corporate Risk Management**, I discuss professionals in corporate risk in Chapter 23 as well as quantitative and quantitative data collection in Chapter 24.

In the seventh and final section of the book, **Pulling Everything Together**, I present some important thoughts as part of the book's conclusion. I have also included some links for further learning as well as a glossary of key terms that I have used throughout this book.

In sum, the seven sections of this book should help you grasp the most important financial risk management fundamentals.

Purpose and Process of Risk Management

CHAPTER 1

WHY I WROTE THIS BOOK

I wrote this book to help individuals learn about the fundamentals of financial risk management, which is one of the cornerstones of finance and economics. I wanted to share what I know and have experienced in a way that could help prepare others to be involved in risk management.

I am particularly pleased to have been able to incorporate both my experiences in directing risk management projects as well as advising corporate clients, industry groups, boards. and executives about interest rate, currency, and commodity risk management.

Those are the big value-add reasons I wrote this book. But on a more pragmatic level, I had already created written materials as part of the preparation to record a course with LinkedIn Learning, *Finance Foundations: Risk Management,* and I was able to combine those writings with some expanded risk topics from my book *Commodity Prices 101*. I believe that this combination of information will be valuable for learners who may prefer to read a book rather than watch online courses.

And why am I the one to write this book?

My background as an economic and financial professional has included several master's degrees, as well as graduate-level courses in economics, finance, and accounting as part of my Master's in Applied Economics and part of an MBA. Plus, I am a Certified Valuation Analyst, Chartered Market Technician, Certified Financial Planner, and Energy Risk Professional. Each of these financial designations has included topics directly related to financial risk management topics.

As for my work experience, I have advised executives on risk management topics for nearly 15 years. I've worked in both investment banking and consulting, and since 2009 I've directly advised senior leaders on financial market risk, corporate risk, economics, and business strategy.

I'm also a financial market expert, and Bloomberg News has ranked me the number one financial market forecaster in the world in over two dozen categories since 2011. I even write on risk and market topics as a columnist for Bloomberg Opinion.

In this book, you'll learn about nine different kinds of financial and non-financial risks that you will then be able to identify and hopefully be able to reduce or mitigate. We will also examine some of the financial risk management solutions like options, swaps, futures, and forwards, that traders and risk managers use to manage their financial market risks. It's important to know what these are and how they work. But don't worry, we won't be doing any crazy math in this course.

In this book, we will also look at how risk management actually works in companies. People talk about risk management, but I give very specific details about collecting and presenting different quantitative and qualitative data. And I discuss some important best practices. By the end of this course, you'll see risks that you might have missed before, and you'll have some idea as to what solutions could be applied. Plus, you'll know how to measure these risks and who needs to monitor these risks and your solutions. In short, you'll know how to spot risks, how to deal with risks, how to measure them, and who to work with to make sure they don't knock your company down.

That is really why I wrote this book: to help people understand the importance, the goals, the process, the fundamentals, and the best practices of financial risk management. Because familiarity with financial risk management topics is not optional for financial professionals. In fact, the future of finance is likely to be dominated by topics and strategies for risk management.

CHAPTER 2

UNDERSTANDING RISK IN CORPORATIONS

Businesses make money because they take risks.

But if they take on too much risk, they could go out of business.

A great example of this is the energy company Enron. It was worth billions of dollars, but the company took on too much risk, and one day the company was gone.

There is an important balance that corporations have to strike between upside and downside risks, and this is one of the core foundations of corporate financial risk management.

Managing risk is important for making a business successful and stable. In this chapter, I discuss how and why risks are important for businesses.

Upside risks present opportunities for profits, but downside risks present the potential for losses.

Effective risk management is important for helping companies both capture the upside opportunities and limit downside risks.

In the same way that a prospector in the gold rush era would have bought a pickax to mine for gold, there was risk involved. Maybe at the end of the day, he would have found gold, or maybe at the end of the day, he would just have a pickax. Any modern business functions under similar conditions.

Businesses take risks all the time to try to capture margin, build their business, drive profits, and achieve growth, and yet if that prospector took everything he had and spent it on that pickax, there wouldn't be much risk management there.

If he doesn't find gold quickly, he could find himself in a very bad place.

Maybe a better strategy would have been to risk a little bit — but not everything. For a corporation, sometimes it's all or nothing, but there should be a good understanding of the risks involved. Knowing the downside risks is a critical first step. You need to know what's at stake.

By and large, entrepreneurs are known as a risk-taking class. Most risk a little at first, until there's evidence that a business can be built, something known as proof of concept. And a proof of concept is when you first prove something can work.

A great example of this was when the Wright brothers tested their first plane in Kitty Hawk, North Carolina.

That plane wasn't the Concord trying to break the sound barrier, nor was it one of *Top Gun*'s F-14s. It was just a wooden plane they were trying to get off the ground for just a few seconds. Now, that short time off the ground provided proof that the concept of flight could work, or the proof of concept.

But even if a business is careful and risks are taken slowly, there are internal and external factors that can threaten to upend almost any business.

There's a joke people like to tell about CEOs, and I've seen it shown in a few different ways, but in each case, the presentation is similar. I've shown an example of this in Figure 2-1.

This kind of graphic shows — as mine does — that the peak goal for most CEOs is to go to Davos, a winter meeting of global leaders, politicians, and cultural icons in the Swiss Alps each January, and while that may be the top goal, the first goal is more fundamental: don't get fired.

For a corporation, the internal and external risks people talk about are not usually focused on finding gold nuggets or going to Davos; they're about going out of business.

When people talk about corporate risk, they're focused on the negative risks that need to be avoided.

Of course, sometimes there is the potential to turn downside risks into upside opportunities, and we'll dig into those in other chapters. But normally when people talk about corporate risk, know that they are talking about minimizing, mitigating, eliminating, offsetting, or otherwise reducing negative risks that could make a company lose money or go out of business.

The way companies do this, the structured way they protect themselves from downside risks, is called risk management.

Figure 2-1

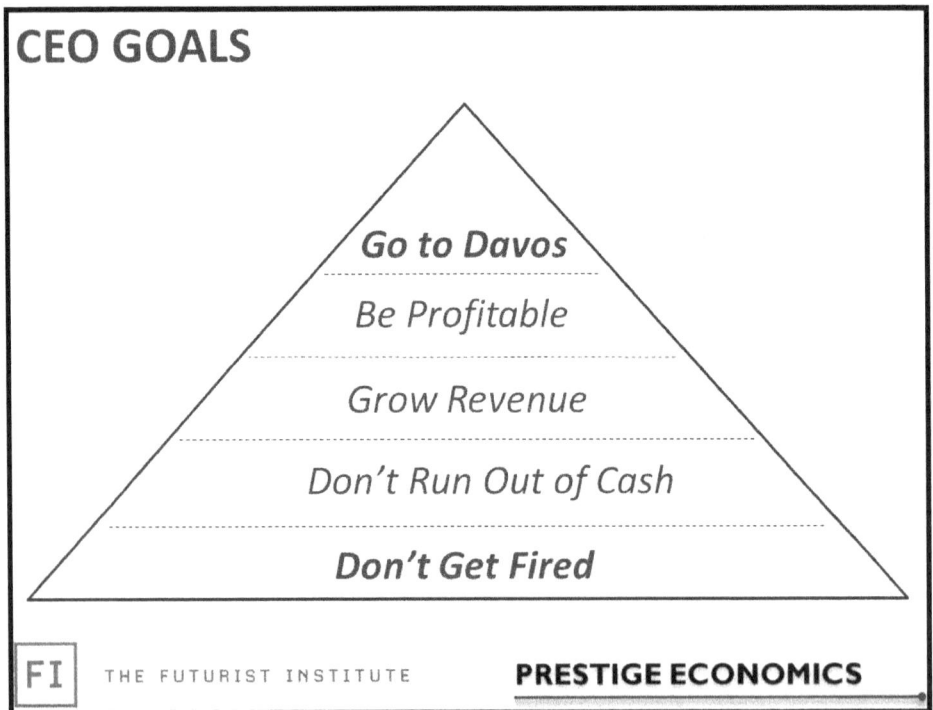

CEO GOALS

Go to Davos

Be Profitable

Grow Revenue

Don't Run Out of Cash

Don't Get Fired

FI THE FUTURIST INSTITUTE   **PRESTIGE ECONOMICS**

So, whether you're a modern-day prospector, an entrepreneur dreaming of flying, a CEO dreaming of Davos, or anyone in between, know that along with the upside risks for your company, there are downside risks that require proper risk management.

CHAPTER 3

RISK MANAGEMENT PROCESS

When I talk to people about corporate risk, most of them want to immediately jump to a topic like hedging without knowing what their risks actually are.

This is like buying racing stripes or spinning rims for a car you don't even own yet. You see, risk management starts not with answers but with questions, and there are three big ones:

- **What are your risks?**
- **What are you going to do about your risks?**
- **Is your strategy effective?**

Let's look at six steps of an effective risk management process:

- **Identifying your risks**
- **Measuring your risks**
- **Owning your risks**
- **Addressing your risks**
- **Implementing your risk management solutions**
- **Monitoring your risk management solutions**

These six steps should answer our three big questions. So, what are your risks?

As you start a risk management project, you need to make sure that you're solving for the right problem. This part of the risk management process includes identifying your risks.

It may seem like a simple thing, but I'll discuss the nine different risks that you need to watch out for later in other chapters. Five are financial, but four are not.

In identifying these risks, you need to make sure the risk management solution you come up with addresses the risks you're trying to contain. Another part of answering the question of what are your risks deals with measuring the risks your business is exposed to.

For example, if you have currency risk in euros because you're a wine importer and you import French wine, it's important to know if you're importing one million euros of wine or 10 millions euros of wine.

Once you know your risks, it's important to know what kind of impact they can have. For financial risks, this is often called the VaR, or value at risk. For example, a 10% rise in the euro against the dollar would cost you an extra million dollars. Now you can answer the first question of a risk management project: what are your risks?

The next big question that logically follows is, what are you going to do about your risks? And the answer could include anything from owning the risk and doing nothing to insuring against the risk by actually using insurance or offsetting the risk with a change in your business model perhaps or with financial instruments like options, futures, and swaps.

Of course, with a mix of different risks your company likely faces, you could end up using more than one of these strategies, and that's okay. It might even take all of these strategies to address the risks your company faces. Now, once you've scoped your risks and decided how you want to manage them, it's time to implement a solution and monitor its performance. Over time, you'll need to ask yourself whether you are managing your risks effectively. And that's the entire goal of risk management.

Interestingly, the answer goes back to the very first things you did, identify and measure your risks. If you identified and measured the risks properly, it should be pretty easy to evaluate the performance of your risk management solutions by going back and doing the math to see if you protected yourself from losses and if you did so in a way that made financial sense. On one level, you might not have managed your risks, suffering a loss, and on another you might have managed them, but you spent too much doing it.

Now that we've talked about the six steps of an effective risk management strategy, can you answer our three big questions from early in this chapter? What are your risks? What are you going to do about your risks? And is your strategy effective?

CHAPTER 4

THE IMPORTANCE OF FOLLOWING A PROCESS

Albert Einstein said, "If I had an hour to solve a problem, I'd spend 55 minutes thinking about the problem, and five minutes thinking about solutions."

This is the reason why the first question of risk management is, what are your risks?

You need to identify the problem before you can solve it.

But you also need to decide on a strategy before jumping into solutions as well. You need to truly know the importance of following a risk management process to build the right solutions.

This is why the order of a risk management process is critical. If you go out of order. implementing an effective risk management solution will become infinitely more difficult and less effective. There's only one order you can go in when implementing a risk management process. You can't leapfrog any steps and expect it to work.

There is a process, and it goes a little something like this. First, you have to start a risk management process by identifying and measuring risks.

This is so you don't waste time trying to fix something that is misspecified. If you have a fleet of cars, you might think crude oil is your problem. But your vehicles probably don't consumer crude oil, they consume gasoline.

That's the problem. That's the risk.

Using financial contracts to manage your risks, in a process known as hedging, with crude oil trading contracts could be part of a solution. But it won't be as perfect as a solution that actually focuses on gasoline exposures. And exposures is just another way for people to talk about unmanaged risks.

After you've identified the risk, you need to get the size right. In this case, it would be gallons. So you need to get right the number of gallons of gasoline that you have as a risk. After all, you don't want to pay for a more expensive solution if you don't need it.

So measure twice and cut once when it comes to risk. If you don't get the sizing and measuring right for risk management, everything else will be off. It will be a series of dominoes falling. And those dominoes could waste your time, potentially creating new risks and maybe even hurting the company you're trying to protect.

Considering your ownership options for the risks you have is next. Before you jump to conclusions about solutions, you need to decide if you want to own certain risks.

Maybe you actually *want* to own some of them.

If your core business function is manufacturing customized stuffed animals, whether you do it in China or the United States may not matter. You probably just don't want to outsource that manufacturing to another company. Even though there may be significant operational risks and challenges.

That being said, if the toy's stuffing is made of cotton, you may wish to address that risk with some kind of a solution, which could include anything from buying cotton fields, storing cotton in bulk when it's cheap, or using a financial hedge on a staggered basis. After deciding what you own, you have to make a decision on how you're going to address the risks that you don't want to own.

Basically, you need to decide what your strategy will be.

Keep in mind, risk management solutions are not impulse buys.

You may decide you need to divest part of your business or put a pricey multiyear financial market solution in place.

Whatever you're planning, don't rush in.

Follow the process, check the numbers, get buy-in, and then proceed.

After all that is done, for goodness' sake, don't just forget about your risk management plan. Check in on it, and make sure to do this repeatedly.

You have to do this.

Otherwise, the financial hedges will expire.

The vehicle fleet could switch to diesel.

And the cotton inventory could fall.

Your risks may shift right underneath you if you're not monitoring your risk management solutions as your business changes. If you follow a structured process in the right order, a corporate risk management solution will be a lot quicker and more effective.

The steps should be done as follows:
1. **Identify your risks**
2. **Measure your risks**
3. **Own your risks**
4. **Address your risks**
5. **Implement your risk management solutions**
6. **Monitor your risk management solutions**

Stay adaptive as needed, but try to get it as close as possible on the first pass. It will save you time, money, and aggravation in the end.

Are you following this kind of structured process in evaluating your risks?

If you're not, then you might be skipping a step, or two, or three.

Four Non-financial Risks

CHAPTER 5

OPERATIONAL RISK

When people talk about corporate finance and the risks companies face, they often think that corporate risks are only financial, but they're not.

Although there is no official number of risks, I believe that businesses face nine different kinds of risks.

Five of the major risks that most businesses face are financial. But four of the major risks — and arguably the most important four — are not financial.

These four non-financial risks companies face include operational, strategic, reputation, and legal or regulatory risks. Let's take a look at each one, and I'll give you some examples to guide you through identifying them in your own company.

The first kind of non-financial risk is operational risk.

This is the risk tied to the day-to-day running of a business and how it might be done wrong.

Think about how lacking antivirus software presents a technology risk. And consider that having bad management could lead to mismanagement or that insufficient controls in quality, environmental, safety, and financial reporting could lead to problems with legal repercussions.

These are all risks from incompetence and people just doing their jobs wrong. These risks require structure in operations and proper leadership.

Although these risks could hurt a company, they're less likely to lead to a company's demise. These are critical areas for improvement that consultants and turnaround firms fix to unlock value from a company that's suffering by having the wrong people, wrong tech, or wrong priorities in place. Basically, these are companies that are just running their businesses wrong.

Questions About Your Company
Throughout the coming chapters of this book about different kinds of risk, I present questions for you to think about your own company's risks.

As they pertain to operational risk, there are two questions to consider about your own company: How is your business run? Are there risks in the day-to-day management, technology, or staff that you can identify?

CHAPTER 6

STRATEGIC RISK

The second kind of non-financial risk is strategic risk.

This occurs because companies don't invest when they need to or they invest when they shouldn't. For companies that don't invest when they need to, they're ignoring something that could hurt them in the long run. If a company holds a strategic position, like say a taxi company before ridesharing came into existence, and they lose their strategic position, the entire business model will suffer.

This is the kind of risk companies face when they talk about disruption.

While taxi companies have seen the value of their medallions and businesses diminish along with their revenues in the face of ridesharing companies, taxis still exist. In more consolidated industries, however, the risk is greater.

Think of how Blockbuster was destroyed by strategic risks it ignored from online streaming, and the move away from brick-and-mortar retail.

In fact, this is something that affects all retail today as the move to e-commerce accelerates.

Strategic risks also face companies when they invest in things that don't work out, like New Coke or Crystal Pepsi. An investment was made, people didn't like the products, and no one bought them. They were just bad investments that lost money.

In other cases, sometimes a strategy is great, but it's just too early, and in that way, it still presents a risk.

Like when there was WiFi on airplanes before tablets and smartphones. That would be a good investment today, but it was too early back in the early 2000s. And it was a bad investment.

These strategies lost money, and these investments maybe should not have been made.

When considering strategic risks, are you ignoring a disruptive change coming to your industry? Or are you making any big investments that might be just too early to market or might not be well received?

CHAPTER 7

REPUTATION RISK

The third kind of non-financial risk is reputation risk.

Reputation is something companies spend years or decades building, but it can vanish in a heartbeat. And this can come in many forms. It can be tied to an individual leader, where an executive is doing something illegal, like stealing money from a company, falsifying financial disclosure documents, or behaving inappropriately.

Reputation can also be tied to a product, like an automotive manufacturer with a parts recall, where faulty brake pads, fuel filters, or airbags threaten the safety of the car users. And it can be affected by a frontline service employee doing something unethical, mean, illegal, or unsavory that reflects badly on an entire brand. Think of someone at a supermarket backdating expired foods. Or mistreatment of passengers on a cruise or airline. These are all significant examples of reputation risks, and although most companies can weather the storm of a reputation risk, the cost in share price for public companies can be high.

In small firms, where reputation is essential, it can be fatal.

Think of a law firm where a partner gets disbarred. Or an asset management firm where a financial planner gets convicted of insider trading or fraud. Bernie Madoff would be a prominent example here.

Are you making sure your people and products convey the right messages and branding?

CHAPTER 8

REGULATORY RISK

The fourth kind of non-financial risk is legal or regulatory risk. This kind of risk can be a godsend or a death sentence to a business overnight.

A subsidy for a wind farm from the government can make that industry profitable, even if the costs exceed revenues in a free market. Or a mandatory inspection of imported toys after an import lead paint scandal could adversely affect the profitability of small importers. A change of labor, environmental, or manufacturing regulations could increase the cost of doing business, and it can do so dramatically, reducing profit margins and potentially putting a company out of business.

Companies face these kinds of regulatory challenges all the time. It's one of the reasons companies spend money on lobbyists to help foster, maintain, and build a legal and regulatory environment that supports their businesses and industries to help their businesses grow. Are you keeping current on potential legal and regulatory changes in your operating territories that could positively or negatively impact your business?

Five Financial Risks

CHAPTER 9

BUSINESS RISK

I know a CEO who likes to say, "You never go broke by making a profit."

When it comes to business, truer words have never been said. But in the quest to make a profit, companies face a number of financial risks — risks that are directly related to turning a profit, managing financial market risks, and having enough cash coming in to keep the business going. In this section, we will take a look at five financial risks companies face. These include business, market, credit, liquidity, and counterparty risks.

I'll walk you through these risks and offer some insights to help you identify them in your own company.

The first kind of financial risk is business risk.

And the first rule of business is buy low and sell high.

After all, that's how you make a profit.

Business risks exist if that isn't possible. Because if you can't make a profit, you simply don't have a business. Of course, a business can lose money for a little while, and it's even expected when a business is starting up.

This is very common among startups and tech companies.

But eventually, businesses need to turn a profit. Without hope of any eminent profits, or any actual current profits, there isn't hope for a business.

Let me tell you a story.

There's a man who sells cars for $25,000, but they cost $30,000 to make. He's losing money on every sale. One day a lady goes up to him and asks how he can do business losing money. And the guy says, "I make it up on volume."

This isn't a real story; it's actually an old joke.

Because you can make up for a narrow profit margin by selling at a greater volume, but there's no offset for a business that loses money on each sale.

It's not what business people call a sustainable model. Which means you'll go out of business pretty quickly, and that's business risk.

Looking at Other Financial Risks

As we look at the other financial risks that businesses face throughout the rest of this book, consider the fact that essentially all risks stem from business risk.

Anything that threatens a company's profitability — that threatens a company's business model of buying low and selling high — is indirectly a business risk. Because increased costs and lower profitability can quickly become a crisis of an existential nature for a corporate entity,

CHAPTER 10

MARKET RISK

The second kind of financial risk is market risk.

Market risks threaten a company because financial markets move because of forces beyond the control of any given company — and those movements can increase operational costs as well as reduce profitability.

The most important financial market risks in the world of corporate finance are interest rate risks, foreign exchange rate risks (or currency risks), and commodity price risks that comes from commodities like oil, corn, and steel.

These risks can drastically affect the profitability of a business. Higher interest rates affect the cost of capital. Currencies can drive up the cost of goods or drive down the sale price. And commodity prices can do the same. They can hurt the ability of a business to buy low and sell high. This is why these risks are the most commonly hedged, to limit costs and to protect profits. I discuss these further in Chapter 14.

CHAPTER 11

CREDIT RISK

The third kind of financial risk is credit risk.

Walt Disney once said, "It's not what you have, but how much you can borrow that's important in business."

Credit is important because it can help keep a business going — and growing.

If a company's perceived corporate creditworthiness falls, the cost of credit for that company will rise. Downgrade risk, which is a big part of credit risk, is the risk that a company will have its perceived corporate rating lowered. And that would be a downgrade.

It's like a company seeing its credit score drop. And a drop in a company's credit score is a downgrade that makes the cost to borrow money rise. This is an important risk to consider internally, because it could cut off access to necessary funds to keep a business going and growing.

In the way that individuals have FICO credit ratings, companies often do as well. And big companies often have ratings for their bonds that are issued by the three large ratings agencies: Standard and Poor's (S&P), Fitch, and Moody's.

The S&P scale, which — in my experience — is the most commonly quoted rating scale, goes from AAA to D. Bonds at or above an S&P rating of BBB– are considered *investment grade*. But bonds with an S&P rating below BBB– are termed *high-yield bonds*, and they are also called *junk bonds*, because their creditworthiness is lower — and the risk is higher.

For Moody's and Fitch, investment grade bonds are rated Baa3 or higher, and high-yield junk bonds are below that level.

By the way, the term *junk bonds* isn't just a term traders use. The US Securities and Exchange Commission defines and discusses high-yield — or junk — bonds here:
https://www.sec.gov/files/ib_high-yield.pdf

Bond prices are determined, in part, by their credit rating. And the lower the credit rating, the higher the interest rate needs to be to attract capital. In other words, if a company has a low credit rating, the cost of capital for that company will be higher. And if one or more of the rating agencies lowers a company's credit rating, the cost of capital will rise.

Of course, rating agencies can also issue credit upgrades for companies, which is when the credit rating goes up — and the cost for a company to issue bonds and attract credit should fall.

As with other kinds of risk, most executives, financiers, and traders are not usually talking about a credit upgrade when they talk about credit risk. It's usually the risk of a low rating or a credit rating downgrade by one or more rating agencies that is encompassed by the term *credit risk*.

For more information on the S&P credit rating scale:
https://www.standardandpoors.com/en_US/web/guest/article/-/view/sourceId/504352

For more information on the Moody's credit rating scale:
https://www.moodys.com/sites/products/ProductAttachments/AP075378_1_1408_KI.pdf

For more information on the Fitch credit rating scale:
https://www.fitchratings.com/site/definitions

CHAPTER 12

LIQUIDITY RISK

The fourth kind of financial risk is liquidity risk.

For a business, liquidity risk is the potential risk that a company could go into default or bankruptcy because it lacks the capital to stay liquid. Because it lacks the cash, or credit, to pay its bills for things like wages, equipment, and other costs.

Companies don't go out of business by issuing too many shares. They go out of business because they have no money and no credit — or they cannot meet their debt obligations. A business needs access to cash and/or credit, and the risk of those going away is a company's liquidity risk.

In order to buy low and sell high, you have to be able to buy low in the first place. Without liquidity, you can't. If you spend too much money on equipment or on a long-term lease for a fancy office, you might not have enough cash on hand to be liquid and keep a business going in the day to day. This is why, in order to keep a business going, you must be liquid.

CHAPTER 13

COUNTERPARTY RISK

The fifth kind of financial risk is counterparty risk.

No matter what strategy you use to manage your risks, if another party is involved, you're counting on them to hold the net if you fall from the trapeze.

They are your counterparty. And the risk that something happens to them is counterparty risk.

If you buy goods or services from a vendor, you have counterparty risks. This is true if you buy insurance, sign a long-term contract, or hedge your risks with a counterparty.

Even when companies hedge their risks, they do it with physical or financial counterparties. This means that counterparty risk can be a very big problem — and it is not as easy to address as many of the other kinds of risk. After all, if you decide to transfer your risk to someone else, and they fail, your risk will neither be diminished, mitigated, or transferred. You will be stuck with it!

An airline might hedge its jet fuel costs in an agreement directly with a refinery.

A car manufacturer might have a long-term agreement with a steel factory.

But if that refinery goes out of business, what would the airline do?

Or if that steel factory goes out of business, what would the auto manufacturer do then?

Banks and Trading Firms as Counterparties

To reduce counterparty risk, a lot of hedging has been done through third parties like banks or merchant traders. Of course, if that kind of hedge counterparty (like a bank) goes out of business, your hedge could be worthless — and it could come undone.

During the Great Recession of 2007 to 2009, when Lehman Brothers went out of business, counterparty risks hit companies that thought they were safe.

One major steel company had responsibly hedged its steel price risks to sell its steel at a high price. But when Lehman went out of business, these hedges evaporated, and it hurt the steel company's bottom line when steel prices fell. Of course, there were other companies that were "out of the money" on hedges with Lehman, and some of them benefited when Lehman folded.

The main takeaway here is this: Choose your vendors and business partners wisely.

Know that if they suffer, you could suffer as well.

How do you feel about the financial and business continuity for your insurance company, bank, vendors, and other counterparties?

Financial Risk Overview

CHAPTER 14

OVERVIEW OF FINANCIAL MARKET RISKS

There are three main financial market risks that can significantly impact a company's bottom line:

- **Interest Rates**
- **Currencies**
- **Commodity Prices**

When these markets move, a company's bottom line can take a hit, and these markets are almost always bigger than the companies they impact because they can be driven by central bank policies, OPEC, and the weather. Interest rate, currency, and commodity price risks are important for the financial stability of a company.

Understanding them will make you interesting at corporate parties, and knowing how these risks impact your business can have a valuable impact on your bottom line.

Interest Rate Risks

Interest rates directly impact the price of money. This means that when interest rates rise, the cost of money goes up, which makes it more expensive for a company to do business.

This change is well out of the control of companies as central banks, like the US Federal Reserve, the Bank of England, and the European Central Bank, determine underlying policy rates that are independent of credit considerations.

Higher interest rates make the debt a company has more expensive to finance.

It's like when the interest rate goes up on your credit card.

Of course, interest rates can also fall, but when we talk about risk, we're talking about the negative risks from higher interest rates, and interest rate risk is how corporate executives describe the potential negative impact if interest rates rise.

Currency Risks or Foreign Exchange Rate Risks

Foreign exchange rates — otherwise known as currency rates — are the rates at which one currency can be traded or exchanged for another. This is like how much a euro costs in dollars or how many Russian rubles you can buy with British pounds or Japanese yen.

Interest rates and central bank policies, as well as national and global economic conditions, drive foreign exchange rates.

Needless to say, these currency drivers are well beyond the control of any individual company, in the same way that interest rates set by central banks are also out of the hands of any individual companies.

While interest rates can drive up the cost of doing business by directly impacting the cost of capital, foreign exchange rates can adversely impact a company's profit margin.

Changes in foreign exchange rates can drive up the cost to buy and import goods — and they can also weigh on the potential sales price of exports.

In other words, as the core business activity of buying low and selling high, a rise in currency rates can force you to buy less low and sell less high.

This can shrink profits and threaten a business.

Currency risk or foreign exchange risk is how corporate executives describe the potential negative impact from a foreign exchange rate move.

Of course there is a risk that currencies could move in your favor, but that isn't what most companies mean when they address their concerns about foreign exchange risk.

Oh, and there two other terms for this risk: FX risk and forex risk. These are shorthand for foreign exchange risk used by corporate risk professionals, executives, and traders alike.

Commodity Price Risks

Commodity price risks are a bit like foreign exchange rates because they impact company profit margins.

Commodity prices come in three main flavors: energy, metals, and agriculture.

Some examples of energy commodities include natural gas, crude oil, and jet fuel. These can be influenced by seasonal demand — like cold weather that drives up natural gas demand in the winter, or the US summer driving season, which is critical for global gasoline and oil demand.

And these can be influenced by government inventory management, like the US Strategic Petroleum Reserve (SPR), as well as by policy decisions from OPEC, the Organization of the Petroleum Exporting Countries.

For metals, there are industrial metals like aluminum, copper, and steel. These can be influenced by growth in China, the strength of the dollar, and global inventory levels. Plus, there are precious metals like gold, silver, and platinum. These can be influenced by central bank reserve purchases or by the purchases of large speculators like hedge funds.

In agriculture, they are grains like corn, wheat, and soybeans, as well as other so-called *soft commodities* like cotton, coffee, and sugar. These are influenced heavily by the weather, but they can also be impacted by trade wars, substitution effects, and biofuel subsidies.

As you can see, commodity markets are influenced by big macro factors that are well out of the hands of companies exposed to the risks.

Furthermore, there are also two sides to each commodity risk, depending on the type of exposure and whether a company is a buyer or a seller. If a company buys commodities, it faces negative risk if the prices of these commodities rise. But if a company sells commodities, it faces positive risks if the prices of these commodities rise.

Risks Out of Your Control
In a world of risks, there are risks you can control and risks you cannot. Financial market risks are almost always naturally out of your control.

In many cases, they're global and just too big. On the upside, however, there are significant and advanced financial risk management solutions to protect companies from these risks.

This is what people are talking about when they speak about hedging. They're buying financial instruments to mitigate or hedge their downside risks, whether they come from a higher cost of capital, a stronger euro, or a weaker oil price.

Knowing what financial market risks look like can help you identify them in your own company. If you borrow money, do business overseas, or buy any commodities, you're likely exposed to financial market risks. What kind of financial market risks does your company face?

CHAPTER 15

DIRECT AND INDIRECT RISKS

Sometimes it's not the devil you know, but it's the devil you don't.

Direct financial market risks are the devils that corporations usually know very well, while indirect risks can be the devils they don't. But those indirect risks need to be recognized, measured, and monitored just as closely as direct risks a company faces.

You need to be able to identify direct and indirect financial market risks, including risks from currencies and physical commodities, and you need to know that these risks can originate from a vendor or a competitor.

Direct Risks

Direct risks are those that a company sees day to day. These risks are tied directly to business operations of a company. The risks do not come through a vendor or a competitor. And they can be both physical and financial risks.

Let's consider a US-based auto manufacturer. As a direct financial risk, a US-based auto manufacturer selling goods into Europe is certain to be aware that a stronger euro would help the company sell more cars into Europe, but a weaker euro would hurt sales.

That's a direct risk — a direct currency risk that the company sees everyday. As a direct physical commodity risk, consider that this auto manufacturer buys steel to manufacture. The auto manufacturer is directly exposed to steel prices. It knows that higher steel prices would erode the profit margin of selling cars. That company sees the direct commodity risk every single day. And the risk comes directly from the business operations.

Indirect Risks

Indirect risks are those that a company does not see day to day, but they can also be currency and commodity risks. As an indirect currency risk, a US-based auto manufacturer may not sell anything into Japan, but that does mean it isn't exposed to moves in the Japanese yen.

If the yen weakens against the dollar, a Japanese competitor could lower its car price in dollar terms to receive the same number of yen. In this way, the Japanese car price would be lower, presenting an indirect risk to the US auto manufacturer.

This is a specific kind of indirect risk. It is an indirect competitor risk. It is also very different from a direct risk like selling cars into Europe and worrying about the value of the euro. This exposure to the yen is something that a company does not see everyday and may not have given much thought to.

Another indirect risk that a company might not give much thought to is indirect commodity risk. An example of this would be if that auto manufacturer buys tires from a vendor. Those tires are made from rubber. If that tire vendor does not manage its rubber price risks, an increase in the price of rubber could drive up the price of tires, which the vendor then passes through to the auto manufacturer. In this way, the auto manufacturer is indirectly exposed to high rubber prices.

This indirect risk comes through a vendor. Without understanding its vendor supply chains and how its vendors manage or do not manage their risks, companies can be exposed.

Now that I've discussed direct and indirect risks, can you name some of the direct currency and commodity risks your company faces? What risks does your company face day to day?

And can you think of indirect risks your company faces from competitors who may be able to more favorably price their goods or services if currency rates move?

What about your supply chain? Do you know about your indirect vendor risks? Do you know how your vendors manage the risks? Do you know how your vendors' vendors manage their price risks? These are second- and third-order indirect supply chain risks.

They can be indirect and easy to miss, but missing them could be costly.

Risk Management Solutions

CHAPTER 16

FINANCIAL RISK MANAGEMENT SOLUTIONS

Companies are up against financial market risks driven by global factors like central banks, OPEC, and the weather.

Understandably, companies want to insulate themselves from these risks, and they use global financial market instruments to do it. Being aware of these risks, and potential risk management solutions, could save your company from a lot of financial pain. Pain that could put a company out of business. This happened to a number of small oil producers when the price of crude oil fell sharply in 2015 and 2016. Companies that didn't hedge their downside oil price risks at a high enough oil price to keep their businesses afloat went bankrupt or were pushed to the edge of bankruptcy.

In this chapter, we'll look at solutions that corporations use to manage their financial market risks and to avoid the pain train that big swings and commodity prices, currency rates, and interest rates can bring.

Corporations manage risks that they don't want to own by hedging them. Hedging is a specific way companies reduce financial market risks by using contracts sometimes called financial market instruments. These instruments are contractual obligations that involve a payout and are dependent on movements in financial markets.

Think of them as a kind of insurance against financial market moves because they transfer risk from one party to another.

These contracts are often provided by banks, trading merchants, and other financial market players. A company that buys aluminum could lose money if the price of aluminum rises. So it hedges that risk using financial market contracts so that it can lock in the price of aluminum at a level it likes. Of course, a company could just buy all the aluminum it will ever need in advance. That would reduce the price risk too, but that strategy could use up all of a company's working capital.

And a company wants its money working, not sitting in inventory in a warehouse. After all, tying up all of its money could eventually force a company out of business.

So another solution is needed.

And that's where hedging comes in. It's a way to reduce your risks at a relatively low cost.

Of course, a good hedge shouldn't present an existential risk to a business the way buying all the aluminum the company will ever need could. All financial market instruments, including options, swaps, futures, and forwards, provide different ways to manage risk.

But they all have one thing in common: two parties. One party is effectively owning the risk, and another is selling it. As such, all solutions unfortunately introduce counterparty risk. And counterparty risk is the risk that a party you have an agreement with could go out of business or otherwise default on its obligations. Since a contract has two sides, you need to believe that the other side is a stable partner. The risk that they are not is counterparty risk.

Your choice. A financial market instrument will likely be dependent on your type of risk, the upfront costs you're willing to pay, and the impact on cash flow you're willing to tolerate. Of course, there are more extreme solutions to manage financial market risks, like making an acquisition (i.e., buying) or divesting (i.e., selling) a business, exiting a market completely, or hoarding the commodity or currency you'll need for many years to come.

These are all usually much more complicated and expensive strategies than using financial market instruments.

But even when managing risks in financial markets, the solutions can be imperfect. And it is critical to monitor how those risk management solutions are performing.

As you can see, financial risk management solutions can be imperfect — and they must be monitored. As noted in Chapters 3 and 4, you need to revisit your risk management strategies. You cannot create them and just walk away. They must be monitored.

Now that you know about major financial and non-financial risks that could threaten your business, let's look at how each of the financial risk management solutions works.

CHAPTER 17

OPTIONS: PUTS AND CALLS

Everyone loves to have options!

But when financial people talk about options, they're talking about financial contracts that give them the right, but not the obligation, to buy a commodity, currency, or interest rate at a specific price.

People love options because they're relatively easy to understand, the cost to use them is clear and upfront, and they are effective tools to help individuals and companies manage financial market risks. Options allow companies to manage risks in foreign exchange rates, commodity prices, and interest rates.

Options are a bit like corporate insurance for financial market risks because risk managers pay an upfront fee to buy options, but also like insurance, options don't always pay out.

And there are two kinds of options: put options and call options.

All options have two parties: a buyer and a seller. They also have a fixed duration before they expire, and they have a price that's important for using or exercising the option. That price is called a strike price, which is agreed upon and set by the two parties.

Both kinds of options also require the buyer of the option to pay the party selling the option (known as the writer of the option) an option premium up front. The option premium is for the option writer to keep, even if the option is never exercised (or used) by the buyer.

Options are called *derivatives* because their value is derived from an underlying security — like oil prices, the euro, or interest rates. Now, let's look at puts and calls.

Puts and Calls
A call option pays the buyer of the option if a market rises. The strike price for a call option is the level at which the option begins to pay out, and it is usually above the market price when the option is purchased.

A call option that pays out for the buyer is *in the money* for the buyer. This is because the option owner will receive funds from the seller if the buyer exercises the option. But when the call is *in the money* for that buyer it is *out of the money* for the seller.

A put option is the opposite of a call option. It pays the buyer of the option if a market falls. The strike price for a put option is the level at which the put begins to pay out. It is usually below the market price when the option is purchased.

As with a call option, a put option that is *in the money* for the buyer is *out of the money* for the seller.

Let me give you a simplified example.

A call option on oil prices with a strike price of $50 pays the call buyer if the oil price rises above $50. Conversely, a put option on oil prices with a strike price of $50 pays the buyer if the oil price falls below $50. This is shown in Figure 17-1.

It should also be noted that a call option on oil with a $50 strike price is not worth anything if oil is below $50 (at $40, for example), while a put option on oil with a strike price of $50 is not worth anything if oil is above $50 (at $60, for example).

Figure 17-1

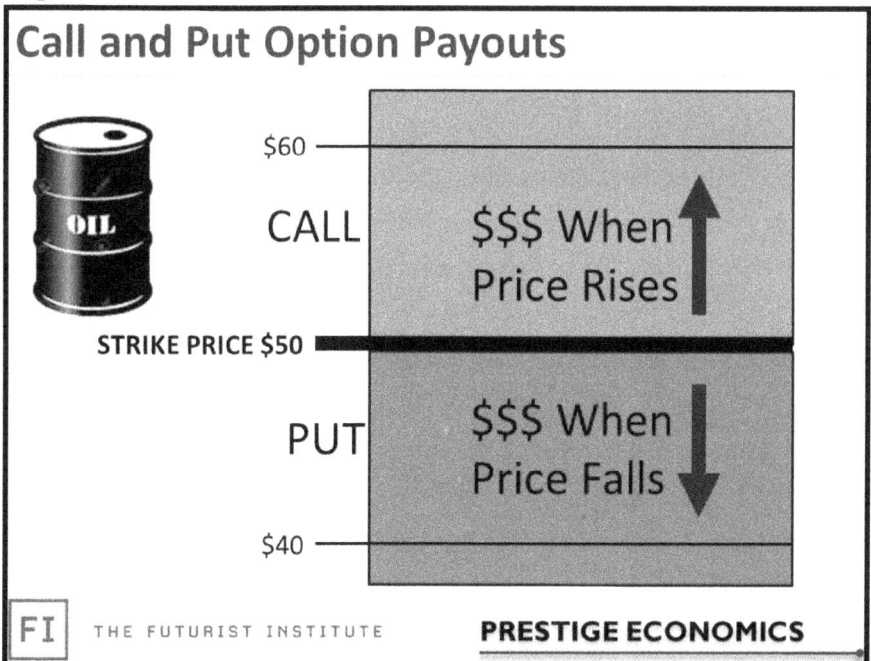

Call and Put Option Payouts

OIL

$60

CALL — $$$ When Price Rises ↑

STRIKE PRICE $50

PUT — $$$ When Price Falls ↓

$40

FI   THE FUTURIST INSTITUTE   **PRESTIGE ECONOMICS**

It also important to know that when the strike price of an option equals the market price, the option is said to be *at the money*.

For the crude oil price call and put in Figure 17-1, a market price of $50 would be *at the money* for both the put and call since they both have a strike price of $50.

Detailed Call Options
Real call options almost never work as cleanly as they do in Figure 17-1.

In Figure 17-2, you can see a more realistic depiction of a call option and how it pays out for a buyer. It's important to note that the option doesn't pay out immediately after a price crosses the strike price, even though the option is said to be *in the money* once a price crosses the strike price, because the cost to buy the option up front — the option premium needs to be recouped before the option is fully *in the money*.

For the seller of a call option, the payout works in the opposite way. After all, the option seller (or writer) gets paid up front to create the option. But if the price of the security goes above the strike price, the option is *in the money* for the buyer of the option and *out of the money* for the seller. Of course, the seller of the option doesn't have a net loss immediately because the seller gets paid up front for the option. Once the price crosses above the strike price, however, the value of that payment erodes, and the net loss to the option writer is realized. This is shown in Figure 17-3.

Figure 17-2

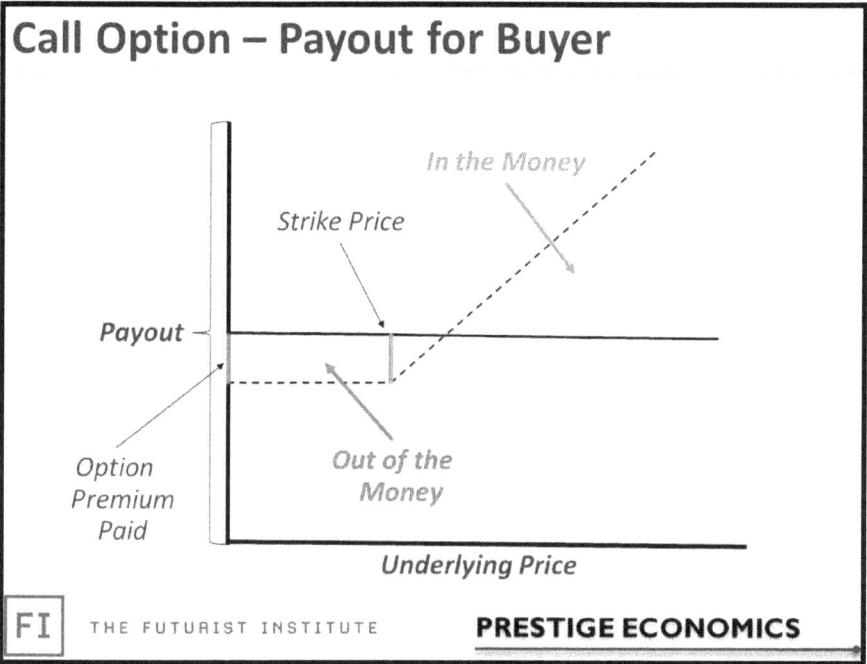

Call Option – Payout for Buyer

In the Money

Strike Price

Payout

Option Premium Paid

Out of the Money

Underlying Price

Figure 17-3

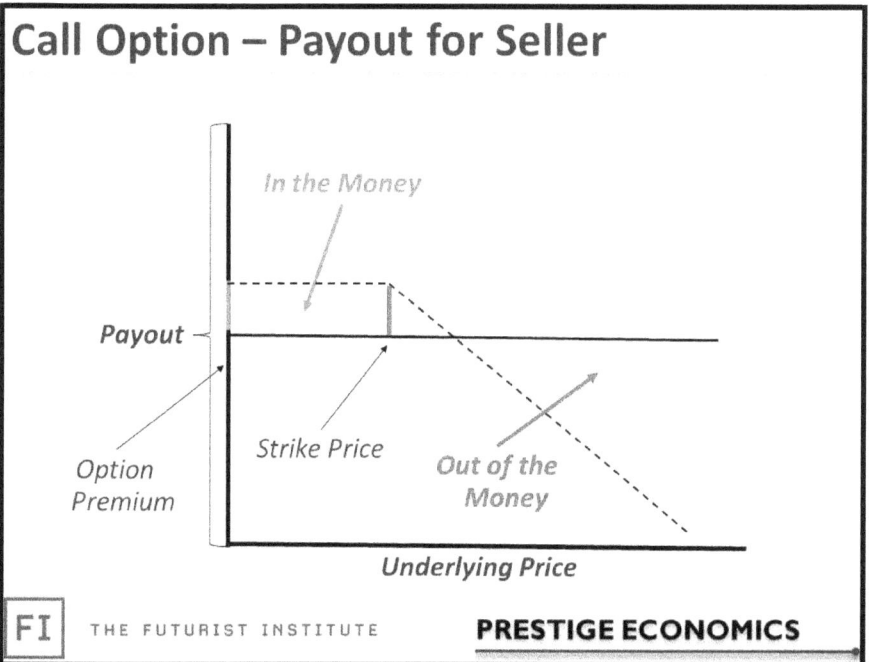

Call Option – Payout for Seller

In the Money

Payout

Option Premium

Strike Price

Out of the Money

Underlying Price

Detailed Put Options

Real put options almost never work as cleanly as they do in Figure 17-1. In Figure 17-4, you can see a more realistic depiction of a put option and how it pays out for a buyer.

As noted above, a put option is the opposite of a call option because it pays the buyer of the option if a market falls below the strike price. The strike price of a put is usually lower than the prevailing market price when the option is bought, which is also the opposite of a call, when the strike price of a call option is usually above the prevailing market price when the call is created. However, as with a call, a bought put does not have a total positive net payout when the price of the underlying asset crosses the strike price because the cost of the option premium needs to be recouped first. You can see the payout for a put option buyer in Figure 17-4.

For the seller of a put option, there is an upfront premium received, and the payout to the put buyer doesn't begin until the price of the underlying security falls below the strike price. And even though a put option is *out of the money* for the seller once the market price crosses below the strike price, the seller of a put option doesn't have a negative payout immediately because of the premium received up front. You can see the payout for a put option seller in Figure 17-5.

Three Kinds of Options

American options can be exercised at any time before expiry. European options can only be exercised at expiry. Asian options depend on the average price of the security over a period of time.

Figure 17-4

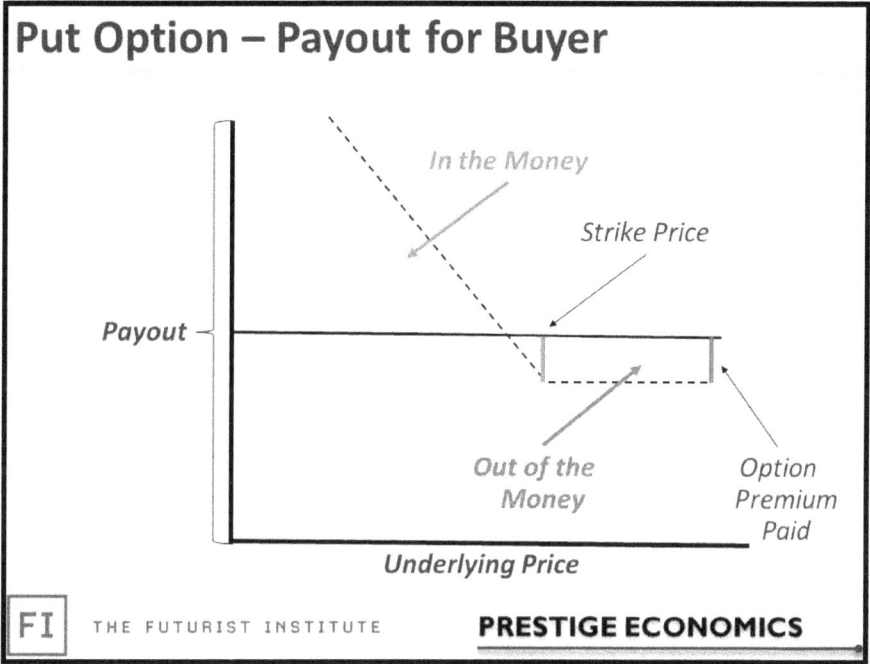

Put Option – Payout for Buyer

In the Money

Strike Price

Payout

Out of the Money

Option Premium Paid

Underlying Price

Figure 17-5

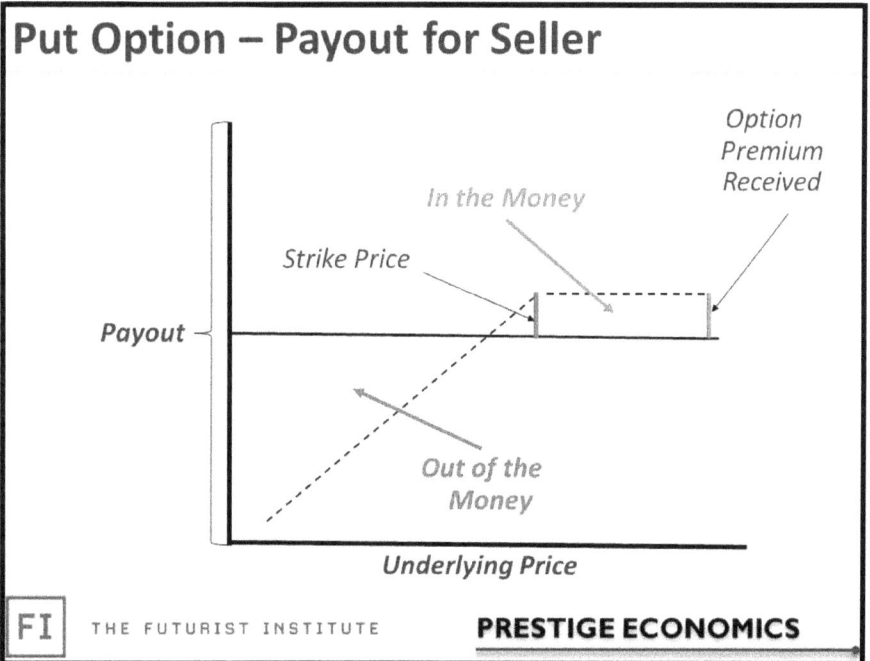

Put Option – Payout for Seller

Option Premium Received

In the Money

Strike Price

Payout

Out of the Money

Underlying Price

It is important to note that American and European options are considered standard options, in contrast to Asian options. And it is important to understand that American options offer much greater flexibility — and therefore greater value — because they can be exercised at any time.

There is one last thing that is important to know about options payouts, which is called put-call parity. This is the theory that a call option and a put option of a certain security with an identical strike price and expiry date have a relationship in their value that is line with the formula **Call — Put = Price — Strike**.

But this formula only works for European options.

The Greeks
The money the company spends on a put or call option is spent, but the risk it is trying to control for is reduced. That should make the company happy.

But even as a company reduces risk using options, it unintentionally adds counterparty risks since the option buyer needs to believe that the seller will be able to pay. Of course, this is less important for the option seller who gets paid upfront by the option buyer.

In addition to counterparty risks that are introduced by using options to manage risk, there are also other risks inherent in using options. These are what risk management professionals, investors, and traders refer to as "The Greeks."

Two Greek letters are commonly used in finance, investing, and trading fields: Alpha and Beta. But these are not just used when using or analyzing options.

Alpha refers to returns that exceed market norms. This is where the publication *Seeking Alpha* derives its name, as a means to achieve excess returns.

Beta refers to investment volatility relative to a broader market, sometimes referred to as systemic market risk.

A Beta of 1 is perfectly correlated with overall market volatility, while a Beta of 0 is uncorrelated and a Beta of –1 is perfectly inversely correlated with broader market dynamics.

Options Greeks

While Alpha and Beta are the Greek letters that represent important ways to talk about financial market dynamics in general, they are not "The Greeks" that refer to financial risk management and options pricing, including Delta, Gamma, Theta, Vega, and Rho.

Delta measures an option's price sensitivity to the value of the underlying asset. For example, this is how the cost of a call option on oil prices would change relative to a change in the price of oil.

Delta is between 0 and 1.0 for call options, reflecting positive correlation price changes in crude oil and the price of oil call options.

However, Delta is between 0 and –1.0 for put options, reflecting an inverse correlation between a drop in the price of oil and an increase in the price of oil put option prices.

Reducing, managing, or hedging risks in Delta to reduce the risk of Delta is called *Delta hedging.*

Vega measures an option's sensitivity to changes in the volatility of the underlying security. Essentially, Vega shows how much the price of an option changes in response to a 1% change in volatility of the underlying market.

For example, the Vega of an LME aluminum price call option will reflect how much an option on LME aluminum will change in response to a 1% change in the price of aluminum.

It should also be noted that with greater time to expiry, there will be a bigger impact of increased volatility on the option's price.

Gamma measures the sensitivity of option prices to changes in Delta. Gamma is used to measure and analyze Delta. And it also reflects how stable the Delta of an option is.

When Gamma is higher, it indicates that Delta could change more significantly if there is even a small change in the value of the underlying security. This is why gamma is higher for options that are at the money but lower for those options that are in the money and out of the money.

Gamma values are also usually lower for options with more time because options with more time to expiry will be less sensitive to changes in Delta.

Gamma values are also usually higher for options with less time because options with less time to expiry will be more sensitive to changes in Delta.

Theta is the trading value placed on time when pricing the value of options. This is also why the term *Theta decay* is used referencing the erosion of value in options, futures, or other derivatives as the date of expiry approaches.

Rho shows how much the price of a derivative changes with a change in the risk-free interest rate.

This can be conceptually reflected as how an option's price would change with a 1 percent change in the risk-free interest rate, which is often reflected by US Treasury Bill rates.

Call options are usually positively correlated with interest rates, while put options are usually negatively correlated with interest rates.

Rho is also more important if an option has a longer time to expiry because interest rate changes have greater impact with a bigger time horizon. Options with a short time to expiry will be less impacted by changes in interest rates.

Considering Your Risks

When managing risks, it is important to understand all of the associated risks, including counterparty risk. For options, it is critical to calculate and monitor *The Greeks.*

Take a moment to consider what markets you would like to hedge with options and at what price level.

What strike price would you set for a call or put option on a financial market risk that you currently have?

CHAPTER 18

INTEREST RATE SWAPS

Have you ever had a risk that you wish you could exchange or swap with someone else?

Well, that's exactly what financial swaps are designed to do for companies. There are a number of swaps for financial markets, but the most commonly used ones are interest rate swaps.

Interest rate increases can have a significant negative impact on a company's cash flow, hurting its ability to be profitable. Interest rates going up is bad for business. If you touch the money in your corporation, you will come face to face with the realities of interest rate swaps at some point in your career.

Almost every corporation uses or considers using interest rate swaps to provide consistent cash flow related to its debt payments.

This is because companies are just like you.

You don't like it when you owe someone money, and it's a surprise that you owed them more than you plan. Companies are the same way. They like to be able to plan for their interest rate risks.

LIBOR
To understand how interest rates swaps work, we first need to talk about corporate debt, which is comprised of two parts: a company-specific interest rate and a rate tied to the cost of money, as set by central banks, known as LIBOR, the London Interbank Offered Rate.

The first part of the interest rate a company pays is tied to a company's individual creditworthiness.

This is like the interest rate on your personal credit card or mortgage that's based on your own personal credit rating. This entity-specific interest rate generally does not change. It is said to be fixed.

The second part of a company's interest rate is tied to the floating market rate for LIBOR, which is related to central bank policy rates.

In the United States, LIBOR is tied to the federal funds rate, which is the main policy rate of the US central bank, called the Federal Reserve or the Fed.

When a company's debt payments change with LIBOR, its interest rates are said to float, because the LIBOR rate can either rise or fall. If LIBOR rises, this part of the corporate interest rate rises. If LIBOR falls, this part of the corporate interest rate falls. Academics call these variable rates, but corporate risk practitioners call these **floating rates**.

Because the interest rate of a company will typically have these two parts, a company rate and LIBOR, the rate of debt is called **LIBOR Plus**, because the rate is LIBOR *plus* the company rate.

This LIBOR Plus interest rate concept is shown graphically in Figure 18-1.

Figure 18-1

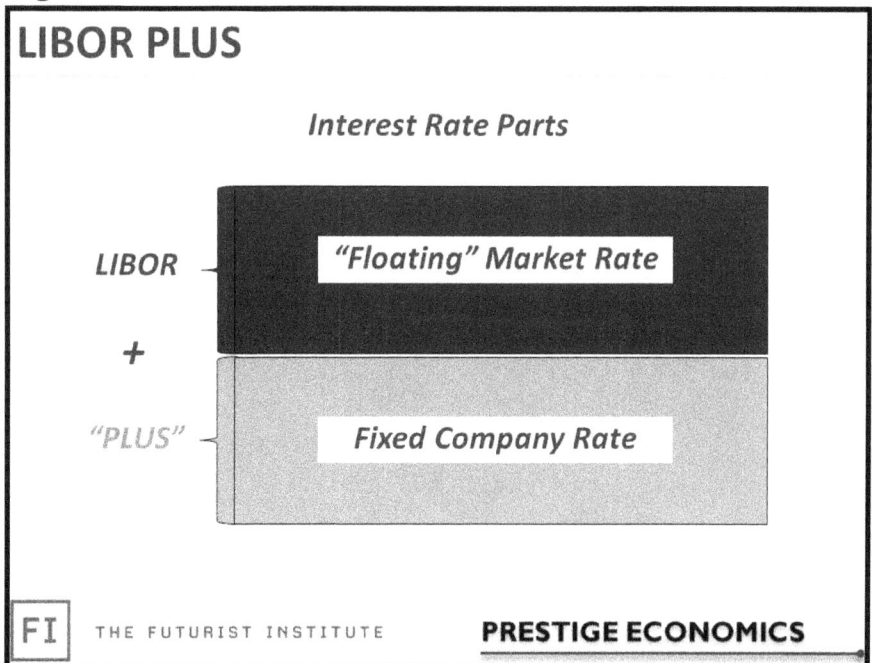

LIBOR PLUS

Interest Rate Parts

LIBOR — "Floating" Market Rate

+

"PLUS" — Fixed Company Rate

FI   THE FUTURIST INSTITUTE   PRESTIGE ECONOMICS

Let me give you an example of a LIBOR Plus rate that you can see in Figure 18-2.

If the creditworthiness of a company results in fixed company interest rate of 5%, and LIBOR is 1%, then the LIBOR Plus rate would be 6%.

If the Fed raises rates and U.S. LIBOR goes to 2%, then LIBOR Plus would be the company's 5% rate plus the 2% rate, so that in total would be 7%.

One thing you need to know about LIBOR, LIBOR rates are usually just a little above federal funds rates, so if the Fed funds rate is 1%, LIBOR might be close to 1.05%.

Figure 18-2

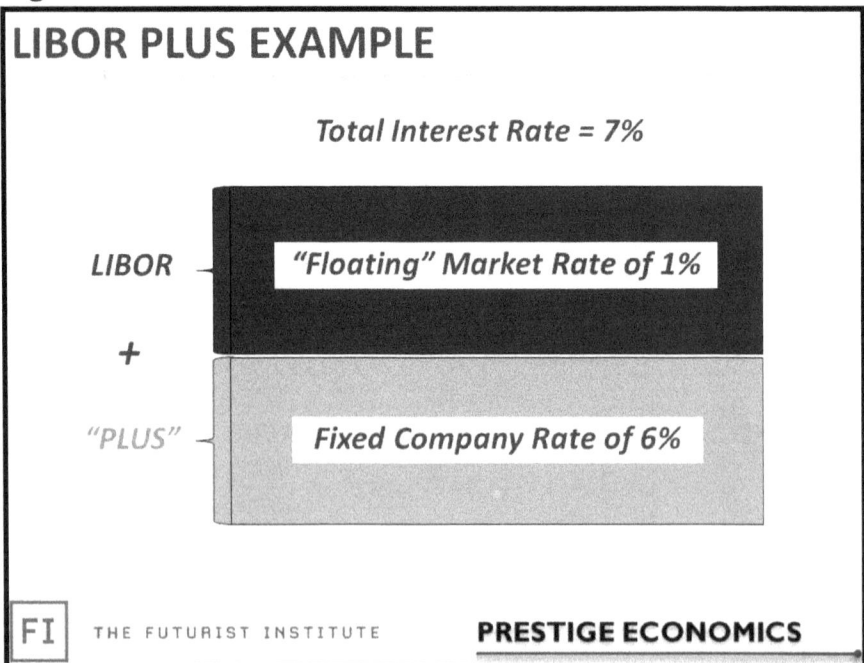

Let's look at another example. If the Fed raises rates from 1% to 2%, LIBOR will likely rise from around 1.05% to around 2.05%. And the cost to pay the interest on the LIBOR part of the debt will rise by 1%.

If a company has a $100 million note, and its payment terms are LIBOR Plus, then each 1% increase in LIBOR rates would make the company's annual interest payment rise by $1 million.

One way to address this risk would be to fix the floating LIBOR part of the interest rate so it doesn't change. This is done by using an interest rate swap, which involves swapping out the floating LIBOR rate for a fixed rate.

One thing you need to know about LIBOR swaps is that when you buy a swap into the future, the interest rate is an average over that time. Since you are locking in your interest rate risks and protecting yourself from higher rates, the interest rate of the swap is usually higher than the current interest rate for LIBOR.

For example, if LIBOR is 1% now but floating and you want to buy a five-year swap, you might have to pay 2% to lock that swap in. And even though the 2% is higher than the current rate of 1%, no matter what happens to LIBOR for the next five years, up or down will no longer matter. You will always pay 2% interest on that portion of the debt.

This means that once the interest rate exposure is fixed with this swap, you will pay a 2% interest rate for the LIBOR Plus portion of the debt servicing even if LIBOR falls or rises, whether it is 0.5% or 3%.

Because interest rate swaps reduce interest rate risks for a company in the future, the company that receives the swap is likely to lose money up front. You need to pay something for reduced future risks. In fact, it's typical for companies to lose money up front in a swap — but at least the company with the swap is hedged against a big interest rate move higher later.

Swaps are Like Mortgage Refis
Because interest rate swaps affect long-term debt covenants, they affect every interest payment a company makes for the life of the swap. In other words, this isn't like a one-time payout from a call or put option.

A swap is like what happens if you refinance your mortgage. You change the interest rate, and that has a long-term impact on payments well into the future.

The reason companies enter into interest rate swaps is to lock in cash flows that go to interest payments.

But sometimes a company can pay more in interest payments under a fixed rate than it would under a floating rate because if LIBOR falls, the company then wouldn't get the benefit from the drop. Its interest rate is fixed whether LIBOR rises or falls.

So, what can you do if you don't want to miss out on the benefit if interest rates fall, but you want to be hedged against a rise in interest rates? Well, there's actually a financial market tool that does that. It's called a swaption.

Swaptions

Swaptions are essentially options to perform a swap. This means that the buyer of the option would have the right — but not the obligation — to engage in a swap in the future if they so desire.

This gives the buyer of the swaption more choice and control. But that doesn't come free. And swaptions are often financed a bit like options, with an upfront payment for the right to do the swap. And then if the swaption is not used, the swap is not implemented. But that is the choice of the party buying the swaption, not the person offering (or writing) the swaption. The party selling the swaption gets the option premium up front.

Questions to Consider

As you can see, there are different ways to address interest rate risks. And in order to get to the right answer, there are a few important questions to consider when addressing your interest rate risks — and what strategies you may wish to implement in order to mitigate your interest rate risks.

Do you know if your company's debt has a floating LIBOR component or if the interest rate payments are all fixed?

Would Fed rate hikes rain on your corporate profits parade? Or is your company indifferent?

CHAPTER 19

FUTURES AND FORWARDS

Would you have been a fortuneteller in a pre-industrialized society?

If not, and if you don't have a working crystal ball, then you might want to lock in your future commodity price risks using commodity futures contracts or forward agreements. Locking in commodity prices in the future allows for future financial transactions that reduce risk.

And this is what many companies do that have commodity price risk exposures.

There are two kinds of agreements you can use:
Futures contracts, which are on an exchange and standardized.
Forward agreements, which are off exchange and customized.

In this chapter, we will look at both of these.

Futures Contracts

Both commodity futures contracts and forward agreements do not require cash outlays upfront. These contracts allow for terms to buy or sell a commodity at some time in the future and are often used for hedging purposes to manage risks.

This applies to energy, agricultural, and industrial metals commodities. Futures are financial contracts with standardized set terms for a commodity that obligates a buyer to purchase the asset or the seller to sell that asset. Futures exist for physical commodities and financial instruments.

Common examples of futures contracts are for crude oil, copper, and cotton. Futures contracts are traded on exchanges. Some of the exchanges you may have heard of include the New York Mercantile Exchange, or the NYMEX, where natural gas and crude oil futures are traded. Also, there's the Commodity Exchange, or the COMEX, where copper futures are traded. Futures contracts include standardized terms of the commodity involved. These terms include quantity, quality, and sometimes geography.

In terms of quantity, futures always include terms that state the amount or volume of goods involved. Like the numbers of barrels of oil, the pounds of aluminum, or the bushels of corn. For instance, an oil driller usually sells oil futures at a fixed price to lock in the sale price of crude oil. And a refinery buys those futures at a fixed price to lock in future costs of oil. Additionally, a corn farmer would sell futures at a fixed future price to lock in the sale price of corn, while a cereal company would buy them to lock in the purchase price of corn.

As for quality, futures contracts also usually include details about the assets involved. This might include gold that is "three nines fine," or 99.9% pure, which is a trading term for 24-karat gold.

Or for crude, it might require to having a certain amount of sulfur and gravity, which are important chemical attributes. And crude futures (as well as others) also include geography terms.

Some futures contracts require physical settlement, while others are settled financially. Let's take the two main traded crude oil contracts.

US West Texas Intermediate Crude Oil (WTI) Futures, and British North Sea Brent Crude Oil Futures.

WTI is physically settled, and WTI futures require that contract buyers receive physical crude oil at Cushing, Oklahoma. If the contract expires and you own it, you're going to get a call to come get your oil.

But not everyone wants that physical risk.

This is why Brent Crude Oil futures can be financially settled.

These contracts do not require buying physical crude oil in the North Sea. You don't have to sport a kilt and show up in Scotland to come get your crude oil. It's all financially settled. One big thing to know about futures is that they are settled on a daily basis. And daily settlement reconciliation can have significant and potentially negative cash-flow implications.

Forward Agreements

Forward agreements, known also as forwards, perform a similar function to futures. But forwards are different from futures, because forwards are customized, off-exchange agreements for one party to buy an asset from another party at some time in the future. Forward contracts are also not settled on a daily basis, but there can be margin requirements.

Every aspect of a forward agreement can be customized, including quantity, quality, geography, and other terms as well.

Some of the examples I've seen of forward agreements that have been created for customized risk management solutions include the following:

- Instead of a NYMEX WTI crude oil futures contract, a forward agreement was set for jet fuel at a certain delivery point targeting delivery at a specific airport.
- Instead of an agricultural contract on an exchange for something like cotton, an agreement was created to hedge price risks for strawberries.
- Instead of a metals contract for gold, an agreement for industrial diamonds was created.

As you can see, these are all a bit more unusual contracts.

And they required forward agreements because the customization of forward agreements is the number one differentiating factor from standardized futures contracts.

Essentially, if there is an energy, metal, or agricultural commodity out there, and it isn't on an exchange, someone somewhere, or more specifically two someones somewhere, probably have a forward agreement in place to manage that more exotic and non-standardized risk.

Futures and forwards are widely used risk management solutions.

Forward Curves

Forward curves are graphical depictions of futures prices in the future. And they tend to take two forms: contango and backwardation.

Contango is the term for when a forward curve shows rising underlying prices in the future. It is considered abnormal for some markets, like oil, because oil supply is generally considered more flexible in the future, which means prices would be more likely to fall. A depiction of a forward curve in contango can be seen in Figure 19-1.

The other main form of a forward curve is backwardation. This means that a forward curve shows that prices of the underlying security are likely to fall in the future. The curve is said to be in backwardation or backwardated. A depiction of a forward curve in backwardation can be seen in Figure 19-2.

When a forward curve reflects future prices of an underlying security that neither rise nor fall, the forward curve is said to be flat.

Figure 19-1

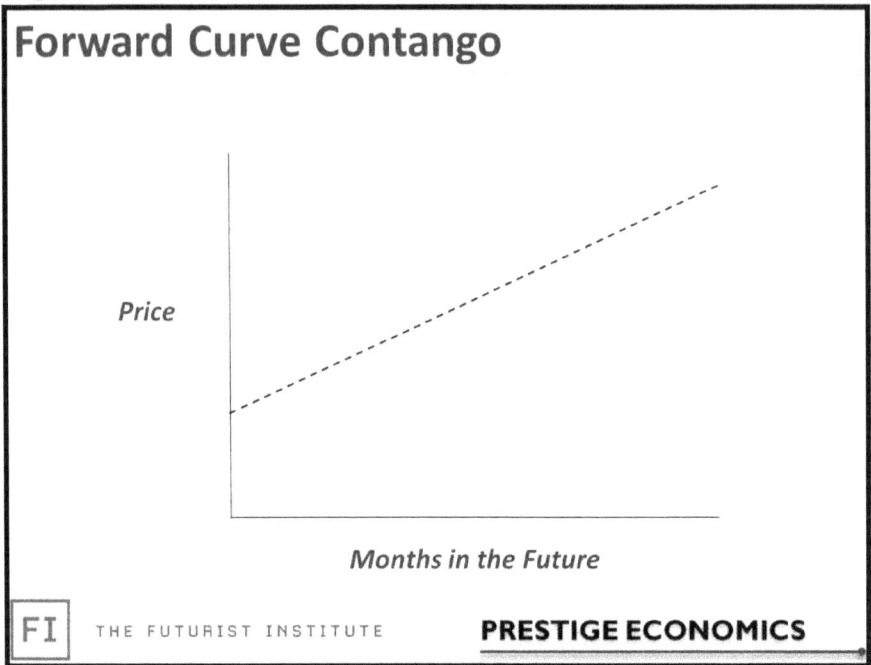

Forward Curve Contango

Price

Months in the Future

Figure 19-2

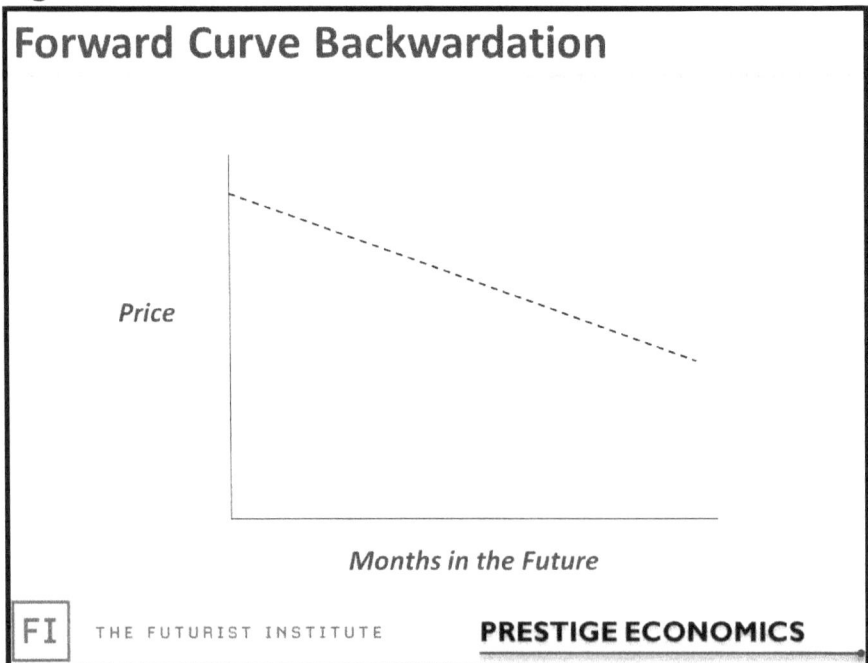

Forward Curve Backwardation

Price

Months in the Future

Of course, not all forward curves are purely in contango or backwardation.

Many forward curves are a mix. In Figure 19-3, I have provided a conceptual example of a NYMEX natural gas price forward curve that shows prices falling into backwardation into spring, when natural gas demand is weak, and then it shows prices rising again into contango ahead of winter and throughout the winter strip. Since natural gas is subject to storage constraints, financial markets can often exhibit time spread differentials that exceed the cost of storage.

There are a few terms to know when talking about the forward curve and commodity prices.

Figure 19-3

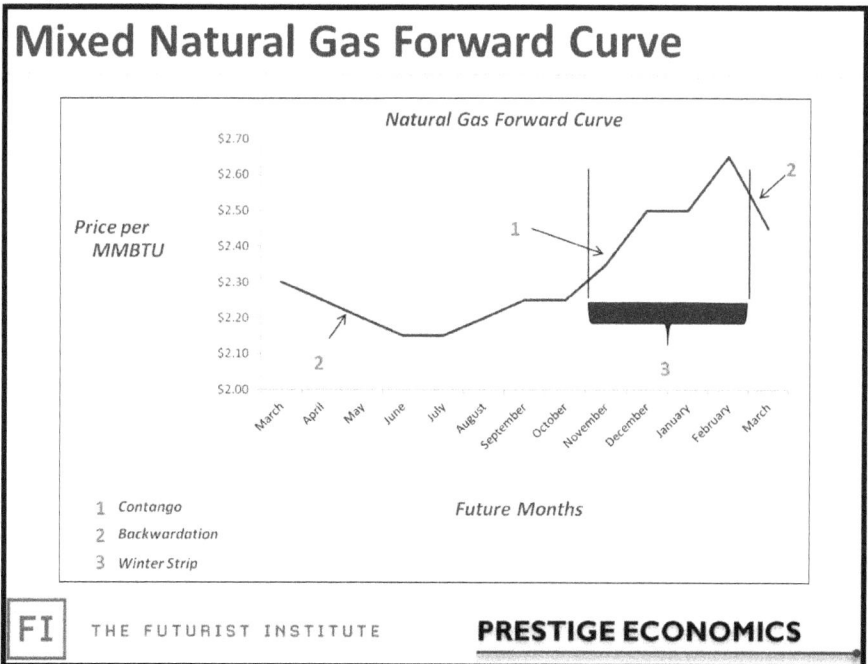

Mixed Natural Gas Forward Curve

Additional Forward Curve Terminology

Although there are a number of risk management terms defined in this book's glossary, there are a number of terms that relate explicitly to the forward curve, which is why they are included in this chapter.

Spot Price — This is the current physical price of a given commodity. This price does not exist on the forward curve but is the actual and current physical price for a commodity at a given delivery point.

Prompt Month Price — The price quoted in the futures market that is the current first contract in the forward curve.

Near-Contract Price — The same as the prompt month price.

Front End of the Curve — This term refers loosely to some of the future contract prices close to the present on the forward curve.

Short End of the Curve — The same meaning as the front end of the curve.

Back End of the Curve — This term refers loosely to some of the future contract prices relatively far from the present on the forward curve. This term is often used to refer to prices far in the future.

Across the Curve — This term refers to price dynamics at many points for contracts on the forward curve.

The Winter Strip — This is a term specific to a seasonally repeating segment of the natural gas forward curve. The winter strip includes points on the forward curve for months of winter trading, when demand is at its peak. The entire natural gas forward curve formation is shaped by this seasonal demand event.

There are, of course, other terms when it comes to discussing the forward curve, but these are the main ones in addition to contango, backwardation, and flat curve shapes.

Forward Curves and Prices

It should be noted that forward curves are historically poor predictors of price. They reflect expectations of future supply and demand as well as the future cost of capital — but they can be greatly influenced by the inherent conservatism of hedgers as well as big price swings engendered by institutional speculators like hedge funds.

Considerations

As you consider the risks your company has, there are two important questions that could determine if a forward agreement or futures contract could be an effective risk management solution:

Does your company have any commodity risks that could be managed with standard futures contracts?

Or does your company have more exotic risks that might require a customized forward agreement?

CHAPTER 20

SOLUTION COST DRIVERS: STANDARDIZATION AND TIME

Nothing is free, and financial risk management solutions can cost a pretty penny.

There are four critical factors that impact the price of a solution:
- **Standardization**
- **Time**
- **Liquidity**
- **Volatility**

Recognizing these four critical factors in different markets will help you understand why they impact risk management solution costs, so let's take a look at them. The mostly commonly hedged financial markets are interest rates, foreign exchange rates, and commodity prices.

And the prices of options, swaps, futures, and forward agreements in these markets are dependent on how standard the markets are, how long you need a solution in place, how liquid those markets are, and how volatile those markets can be.

The first two of these factors that impact price, standardization and time, are pretty straightforward.

Standardization

Standardization is simply how common the requirements for the risk management solutions are.

If you can manage your risks by accessing a broadly or deeply traded market, then there are contracts traded on an exchange.

It can be done a lot cheaper than a solution with a unique set of requirements. But sometimes you want to manage risks that don't exactly match up with a standardized contract that you'd find on a trading exchange.

This is usually because you have one of three differences in the types of risks you face compared to those standard contracts on an exchange.

And these three differences are likely to be in **product**, **timing**, or **geography**. These differences create something called basis risk, because you want to manage the risks of something that is different from the basis for the standard solution.

The more basis risk you have, the more expensive the solutions will be.

Simply put, if you want something custom, it will cost more.

For example, if you want West Texas Intermediate crude oil delivered to Cushing, Oklahoma, in December five years from now and you want to be assured of a price, that will be easy since there's a futures contract trading on the New York Mercantile Exchange, the NYMEX, *right now*, exactly for that.

If, however, you want to lock in the price of a less liquid product, like jet fuel prices in the Atlanta area during a certain three-week period, that solution is going to be more expensive.

There are customized parts of that risk for geography, timing, and product type.

To go back to our fuel example, the NYMEX WTI crude oil contract in Cushing in December five years from now is a standard contract, whereas that Alaskan jet fuel solution is not.

In this case, the basis risk for that contract is high because there's customization requirements in all three standardization risk categories: product, location, and timing.

This will make the cost of the solution more expensive because it will require something off exchange.

Furthermore, and more importantly, nonstandard risks will not mirror exactly what is traded in a standardized contract on an exchange.

Time

The second fairly straightforward factor that affects the prices of risk management solutions is time. Time for risk management contracts represents the time until they expire, which is often called the time to expiry.

The closer the hedging contract is to its expiration, the cheaper it is. Traders and hedgers refer to this as theta.

As time passes, a risk contract loses some of its value because there is less flexibility in terms of when you can exercise that contract.

As I mentioned in Chapter 17, that loss of value is called *Theta decay*.

If you want to hedge Japanese yen five years from now at a certain rate, the solution will be much more expensive than if you want to hedge Japanese yen for five days from now.

And the same is true across commodities, currencies, interest rates, and other financial market risks.

In essence, time is money!

This means that an agreement with more flexibility of time is generally more valuable and therefore, logically, more expensive. As you can see, the importance of standardization and time attributes for the cost of financial risk management solutions is pretty straightforward.

When it comes to standardization and time, more customized solutions cost more, and solutions that protect you for longer are more expensive.

The concepts of liquidity and market volatility are more complicated but equally important. We will discuss those in the next chapter.

CHAPTER 21

SOLUTION COST DRIVERS: LIQUIDITY AND VOLATILITY

There are four factors that determine the cost of a financial risk management solution:

- **Standardization**
- **Time**
- **Liquidity**
- **Volatility**

I covered standardization and time in Chapter 18. And they're pretty straightforward.

But liquidity and market volatility are two other important parts of pricing, and they're a bit more complicated.

Liquidity

First, there's liquidity in the market, or how easy it is to transact. And there's market volatility, which represents how big the swings are in a given market, both up and down.

Let's look a little bit deeper into these two factors and how they are related.

Markets that have more transactions and more market participants are said to be more liquid. And that makes it less expensive to trade in those kinds of markets.

For example, US dollars are more liquid to trade than British pounds. And British pounds are more liquid than Polish zloty. The more liquid the market, the less expensive the relative cost of the risk management solution.

There are a couple of reasons why less liquid markets are more expensive.

First, a less liquid market is likely to have a higher rate of implied volatility, which impacts pricing for models in hedging.

Second, lower liquidity usually also shows up in the bid-ask spread, which is the difference between what people buying in a market are willing to pay, which is called the bid, and what people selling in a market are willing to accept, the ask.

The deeper a market, the more liquid it is, the narrower that bid-ask spread will likely be, and the lower the volatility will be.

In sum, hedging financial market risks in more liquid markets is easier and less risky, and therefore is cheaper than hedging risks in less liquid financial markets.

Let's look at a currency example.

The British pound and the euro have narrow bid-ask spreads that often go out to the fourth decimal. As in the price of euro in dollars for $1.16 would be quoted at the third and fourth digits. For example, the 1.16 euro would be quoted at 1.1681. You've got to go out four decimal places in order to get to the bid-ask spread.

That's how liquid that market is.

In other words, the transaction cost, that difference between the bid-ask spread, is narrow because it's easy to transact in this market since it's liquid and there are a lot of players in the market at any time.

And that makes it a deep market. Plus, currencies like the euro typically will have lower levels of volatility because they are considered broad and deep. You want that narrow bid-ask spread because it makes it a solution cheaper.

But a less liquid currency will have wider bid-ask spreads, and they're also likely to be exposed to higher levels of market volatility. Bigger swings, both up and down. Thinly traded currencies are also referred to as exotic currencies and include the Jordanian dinar and the Belarusian ruble.

They have very wide bid-ask spreads and are not traded anywhere near the same frequency or volume as the euro, the Japanese yen, the British pound, or the US dollar.

As such, it's more difficult and therefore more expensive to hedge risks in these kinds of exotic currencies.

Interest rates are also like currencies.

More liquid interest rates risks are easier to hedge. US Treasuries and German Bunds are liquid, while Moroccan or Uzbek debt are less liquid.

As such, Treasuries and Bunds have narrower bid-ask spreads and likely, lower volatility, which makes them relatively easier and cheaper to buy, sell, or use as hedging instruments. Finally, much like currencies and interest rates, the most commonly traded commodities, like gold and silver, also have narrower bid-ask spreads.

Less liquid commodities markets, like propane and rubber, are more expensive to hedge. Plus, there can be very big price swings in less liquid commodity markets.

This is why oil is cheaper and easier to hedge than jet fuel. Oil is more abundant and has a broader market of trading than just jet fuel. As such, crude oil bid-ask spreads are significantly more narrow than jet. A liquid market is cheaper to transact in, and an illiquid market's solution will always be more expensive.

After all, less liquid markets can also experience higher levels of volatility.

Volatility

In addition to liquidity, market volatility is also a critical factor that determines the price of risk management solutions.

In general, if a market is more volatile and it has bigger swings, buying a financial instrument to protect against that risk will be logically more expensive.

As part of a means to incorporate volatility risks, options pricing models incorporate something called implied volatility or implied vol. This is a measure of how volatile the market is — and it needs to be priced into risk management solutions.

More volatile financial market risks will be more expensive to hedge than less volatile markets.

And volatility often goes hand in hand with liquidity.

That's why these two critical risk factors impact risk management solution prices in tandem.

CHAPTER 22

NON-FINANCIAL SOLUTIONS

When thinking about financial market risk management, the first instinct of some is to jump into financial market solutions.

But there are usually other solutions, including natural hedges, physical agreements, acquisitions, and divestitures, that could provide the same level of protection or better, ways that companies can also reduce their financial market risks without using options, swaps, forwards, or futures.

These are more operational in nature, but they can get the job done.

Natural Hedges

One of the simplest ways to manage a financial market risk is to use a natural hedge, a hedge that exists within your business operations. This is a strategy that relies on taking advantage of risks within a business operation in order to cancel out some of those risks or create flexibility.

For example, if you have euro exposures but you're a US-based business, maybe you want to reinvest the euros in Europe when that currency is weak and you can build your business in Europe. This would allow your company to repatriate its earnings to bring them back to the United Stated in dollars whenever it wants.

When the euro is strong, you could quickly ship them to the United States and convert them into dollars, but when the euro is weak, you might want to leave your profits there and let them feed a growing European business. Another way to tackle the problem is to contractually push the risk onto someone else's plate.

You could also make vendors or customers absorb the risks.

This is also a way of transferring risk away from your company or business.

Transferring Risk to Vendors or Customers
Or you could use a long-term agreement to lock in the price of a certain aluminum extrusion or a certain amount of copper wire. In that case, your vendor is responsible for the market risk, not you.

You could do the same with customers and lock them in with long-term agreements to buy your tractors in euros rather than in dollars even though they might be in the United States.

There are, however, risks to locking in long-term prices; if markets move in your favor for example, you won't be able to get that benefit if things are already set in stone. Plus, long-term agreements will still have an expiration date, and counterparties might not want to sign such agreements at all.

If your counterparties, like vendors, won't sign long-term agreements, then maybe you can actively push on them to manage their risks. For example, if you're a large auto manufacturer that buys tires for your cars, and you love these tires, but the lack of risk management of your tire vendor drives you crazy, you might be able to use your leverage as a big customer to get the tire vendor to better manage its rubber risks.

There are also two other risk management solutions to consider, but they're a bit more extreme.

Acquisition and Divestiture

Acquisition and divestiture. On the one hand, you could make an acquisition to buy a business in order to improve a risk management solution. Your auto company could just buy the tire company outright and implement its own risk management solution to reduce rubber price risks.

This could prove to be a good risk-reducing strategic acquisition, but it's a much bigger decision.

It requires a much bigger commitment than transferring your risks to a vendor or finding a natural hedge.

There could be issues to contend with. Will you still be able to sell those tires to your competitors? Another similarly large decision would be a divestiture, selling a business.

If you have business operations in Thailand, but the exotic Thai bhat is too volatile a currency for you to manage actively, you could simply divest or sell your operations there.

You could set up shop in a country with a more liquid currency market for hedging, but as with an acquisition, a divestiture is a very big decision and one that usually eclipses currency risk in terms of its importance for a business's operations.

After all, divesting of your operations in a region or country could dramatically impact your business. Plus, chances are there were more important strategic reasons than currency risk why you put your operations in Thailand, like the cost of labor, geographic location, access to markets, and other factors.

Recap

You don't need to go to financial markets for the only solutions to manage, mitigate, or reduce your financial risks.

You could find a natural hedge, push the risks to someone else, make an acquisition, or make a divestiture.

All of these different strategies, however, are more complicated and require more approvals as well as a much greater level of corporate commitment than implementing most financial market risk management strategies.

There is also one other important consideration about risk ownership.

If none of these non-financial risk mitigation strategies appeal to you, you could also simply decide to own your risks because maybe you like the state of the corporate risks at hand — either because you see them as advantageous or insignificant.

In that case, no hedge or risk management solution would be necessary.

Corporate Risk Management

CHAPTER 23

PROFESSIONALS IN CORPORATE RISK MANAGEMENT

There are people behind the words *risk management.*

After all, risks don't monitor and manage themselves.

Most professionals involved with corporate risk management have a high level of numeracy, curiosity, and a desire to get to the bottom of things. Corporate financial and non-financial risks require active risk management from risk managers, risk committees, executives, and advisors dedicated to confronting risk.

In business we talk about market drivers as fear and greed, about a big sack of money and a big sack of money on fire.

If you're in risk management, you're usually looking out for the big sack of money that could catch fire. In this chapter, we will dig into the execution of risk management solutions, including the corporate players who actually monitor and manage risks.

The second critical element of independence is the **independence in appearance.**

The goals of risk management professionals in a corporate organization are to monitor, measure, and actively manage risks. Part of this is to make sure that current risks are being watched and future risks are being watched out for.

Risk management within corporations has three main internal players: risk managers, risk committees, and C-level executives. There are also external advisors who can support corporate entities. Risk managers are employees whose day-to-day roles involve monitoring and managing risks. If you work in agriculture, they might be writing reports about rainfall. But if you're a construction company in California, they might be monitoring buildings for earthquake resistance.

Risk manager roles and responsibilities may include producing reports and performing analysis on any number of risks that a company faces, both financial and non-financial.

Risk manager responsibilities may also include monitoring open trading positions, trading, and actively managing risks by working with external counterparties to buy options, manage swaps, futures, or forwards.

Risk committees can be formal or informal groups of corporate employees who are exposed to risk in their day-to-day roles.

They may also be employees with specialized knowledge, in an area like energy prices.

Or they may be dedicated to the oversight of risk in a particular region, like Africa.

These committees can be housed in one dedicated division of a company, or the committee can be comprised of people from different groups who are dispersed throughout an entire organization.

When I worked in banking, there were risk committees in each of the different departments that met regularly, sometimes weekly, and there was one major and senior corporate risk committee that met once a month or less.

In companies that formally address risks and have risk management strategies, risk committees can drive specific decisions about how to manage corporate exposures, like if electricity prices should be hedged.

If they are focused on metals prices, they may manage position limits, like how many tons of aluminum should be locked in with a swap. They could manage pricing, like agreeing on a preferred buying or selling price for an option, swap, or other solution.

And they could manage timing, like when contracts need to be executed and set with a certain expiration.

The closer the committee is to the tactical implementation of strategy, the more frequently it should meet.

Those committees that address more long-term strategic risks meet less frequently, unless a crisis is looming. Risk executives are not found in all companies. Some companies have a dedicated CRO or Chief Risk Officer, who will have risk managers as direct reports. Those subordinated managers may monitor country risk, currency risk, commodity risk, or any other kind of risk.

But more often than not, the executive role of risk management falls by default to the CFO or Chief Financial Officer of a company. In the absence of a CRO, and given that corporate risks can adversely affect the bottom line of a company, the CFO is usually responsible as he or she signs the financial filings and reports of a company.

While having a CRO is a best practice, there is a significant cost and commitment to risk management required. As such, most companies forego this position.

Beyond internal institutional risk management knowledge and professionals, what we find is that there are also roles and responsibilities that corporate boards fill to advise their CEOs directly. This is because risk topics of governance, markets, technology (including cybersecurity), and operations are often part of a corporate board's mandate.

After all, these risks that corporate boards focus on can often be going concern issues.

In addition to the internal risk management resources a company allocates to addressing and monitoring risk issues, external advisors and consultants can also provide risk management support to a corporate entity.

Companies monitor and manage their risks in a number of different ways, and there are professionals that address these risks as part of their formal full-time roles, part-time committee participation, internal and executive capacities, and in external advisory roles.

Can you name the people on the risk committees in your organization or the person at the top of the risk food chain?

Is it a Chief Risk Officer (CRO) or Chief Financial Officer (CFO)?

Or is this an area where you think oversight and corporate attention is lacking?

Is your company's sack of money at risk of catching on fire?

CHAPTER 24

QUANTITATIVE AND QUALITATIVE DATA COLLECTION

We've looked at risks and risk management solutions.

Now you probably want to know how people actually manage risks in their day-to-day jobs.

Risk managers, committees, executives, and advisors monitor risks using a process, metrics, and data.

In this chapter, we'll discuss the hands-on process that risk professionals use to monitor and manage various financial and non-financial risks. Risk management professionals use a mix of quantitative and qualitative tools to monitor risks.

Some of it's based on hard numbers, but some of it's based on research designed around the concept that *data* is really just the *plural of anecdote.*

Before risk assessments are made, risk managers pull together all the data that matters.

Quantitative Data Collection

Quantitative data are taken from financial markets and are based on predictive correlations, or they may come from government sources. Let's look at three examples of risk that managers are using in a quantitative way.

First, a country risk manager is very concerned with the level of currency rates. Major moves present big risks, and these will be collected and presented in a report.

Second, a commodity risk manager that's responsible for heating a number of buildings in the winter will be watching the temperature and is likely to use a statistical program to analyze the relationship between cold weather and natural gas consumption and prices.

Finally, a risk manager tasked with monitoring an industry or economy will be watching government data about gross domestic product, housing starts, or manufacturing to report on whether an economy, or sector in the economy, is growing or in recession.

Qualitative Risks

Now, qualitative data are not hard numbers. These are compiled from anecdotes, the media, and open sources. Or they can be derived from something called "HUMINT," which is human-intelligence-derived data. This is the type of research that some strategy organizations, hedge funds, and intelligence organizations conduct in order to achieve unique and high-value insights that are not easily identified.

Even my company, Prestige Economics, collects a quarterly survey about growth and risks. We ask dozens of executives what they expect, and we compare these results to the relationship with growth in past quarters. We have found tremendous value in collecting this kind of data over time. In fact, some of the data from our surveys directly impact our economic and financial market forecasts.

Additionally, some equity analysts make trade recommendations and put stop-loss positions on based on the number of times a company's name has been tweeted.

Plus, there are some companies that trade, buy, or sell crude oil or industrial metals prices that may have people literally sitting in small boats in a harbor with binoculars, counting the number of ships carrying crude oil, jet fuel, iron ore, or steel arriving at a certain Chinese port or departing from it.

The thing is, each company's quantitative and qualitative data to watch are different. But the types of data should be directly related to the risks involved. And they should have some statistical and predictive relationship that's been tested and proven over time. And most risk management assessments are a mix of quantitative and qualitative risks.

For example, although currency risk is a top priority for country risk, the reality is that country risk monitoring includes both quantitative and qualitative risks. And qualitative risks are critical for country risk. These include a country's political stability, geopolitical alliances, and its regulatory risks.

Qualitative risks for a company can be equally important. These often involve looking at the non-financial risks of a company, including the company leadership, organization structure, and business model.

Quantitative Risks

Quantitative risks are all numerical or statistical. And they can include currency moves, capital markets, and sovereign debt rates, while qualitative risks include political, geopolitical, and regulatory risks.

Once all of the right data — both qualitative and quantitative data — have been collected, risk managers pull it all together to present potential implications in reports. And these reports usually break down risks by type, region, probability, and financial implications.

The most important financial measure of corporate risk is called value at risk, or VaR for short. VaR represents how much value could be lost in any number of different scenarios. Most risk reports attempt to capture VaR, even if the risks involved are not easily quantified.

Often, risk professionals might create a heatmap to show big risks as red, medium risks as yellow or orange, and low risks as green. This assessment is often qualitative and based on the professional experience of the risk manager.

In some cases, it may be driven by equations and hard numbers.

But in some cases, it may not.

For example, an airline monitors the VaR of jet fuel prices, how much the airline could gain or lose for various prices of jet fuel along a distribution of potential prices. In addition to VaR, risk managers and committees monitor the nine financial and non-financial risks. Reports prepared by risk managers for country risk, indirect vendor risks, and regulatory risks usually also include a description and evaluation of current strategies to address these risks, like hedging, new vendor identification, and government lobbying.

After the data is pulled together, risk management committees review the data analysis and reports prepared by risk managers. And executives, like a CRO, CFO, or CEO, review the committee's conclusions. These executives may also seek the advice of the corporate board, external advisors, or consultants to assess and manage these risks.

VaRs of all kinds must be constantly monitored, and risk management solutions must be monitored for effectiveness. These are critical parts of an effective risk management process.

What quantitative and qualitative factors do you think would have important implications for the major risks your company faces? How often do you think those risks should be monitored?

Pulling Everything Together

FINANCIAL RISK MANAGEMENT FUNDAMENTALS

Thank you for reading this book on financial risk management fundamentals.

In this book, we've looked at the nine different kinds of financial and non-financial risks. Now you should be able to identify these risks whenever you come across them in the business you work for, a business you might work for in the future, a business you might start for yourself, or a business you want to invest in.

We also looked at important financial risk management solutions, including options, swaps, futures, and forwards.

Traders and risk managers use these solutions to manage their financial market risks, and you should now be familiar with the basics of these important and complicated solution. But not all risks are financial, and there are also a number of non-financial risk management solutions that can be implemented to protect your business.

Finally, we looked at how risk management actually works in companies.

A lot of people talk about risk management in theoretical terms, but I think it is critical to look at very concrete examples when describing the best practices for collecting and presenting quantitative and qualitative data for risk analysis. And I hope this approach has instilled a deeper level of risk management understanding — and creates new professional opportunities for you.

Now that you've read this book, you'll likely see risks that you might have missed before, and you should have some idea as to what solutions could be applied.

Plus, you know how to measure these risks and who needs to monitor them.

Look around at your company's risks.

I'm sure that you see some that are being addressed and others that are being overlooked, and this is where you can add tremendous value to your organization, by thinking about and talking about risks before they become a problem.

Further Learning
If you've enjoyed this book and want to learn more about risk management, you can start by taking my LinkedIn Learning course on *Finance Foundations: Risk Management.*

Here is the link to that course: https://www.linkedin.com/learning/finance-foundations-risk-management

If you want to know more about how you can build a career as a risk professional, take a look at the events and information on the website for GARP, the Global Association of Risk Professionals, at www.garp.org.

You can also check out PRMIA, the Professional Risk Managers International Association, at www. prmia.org.

On these sites, you'll find plenty of opportunities to learn more about risk management, and you'll have the opportunity to network with professionals who are active in the space. Now you know how to spot risks, how to measure them, how to deal with them, and who to work with to make sure they don't knock your company down. Your company needs to be a big sack of money, not a big sack of money on fire.

And you can help make that happen.

FINANCIAL RISK MANAGEMENT GLOSSARY

At the Money — When an option is not in a position to pay out for either party, because the underlying price is equal to the strike price. This means it is neither "in the money" nor "out of the money" for either party.

Business Risk — Critical non-financial risk that a business is not profitable. This is often due to the fact that a business model is not sound.

Call — A financial derivatives instrument that derives its value from an underlying security. A call is paid for upfront with an option premium, and it is sold by an option writer. If the price of the underlying security is *above* the strike price, the call is said to be in the money for the buyer of the call option. Calls are often used as hedges against upside price risks as they pay out to the buyers if prices rise. Calls are the inverse of puts.

Counterparty Risk — Risk introduced by working with another party. This financial risk can be introduced when trying to mitigate other risks.

Credit Risk — Risk that a company may not have access to credit to finance its operations. Credit risk could be tied to an inability to access credit as well as to an increase cost of credit, due to a rise in LIBOR and other underlying interest rates, as well as to risks posed by a potential credit downgrade.

Derivatives — Financial securities that derive their value from an underlying security. Derivatives include puts, calls, options, swaps, and swaptions.

Direct Risk — Financial and non-financial risks that a company is directly exposed to through its own operations.

Downgrade Risk — Risk that a company's credit rating will be lowered, thereby increasing its cost of capital and increasing the difficulty it may have in accessing credit. Rating agencies provide ratings of corporate bonds.

Forward Contracts — Financial derivative instruments used for risk management purposes, which are often customized and created off exchange. Forwards are fixed commitments to buy or sell specific underlying securities at a future time. These are also sometimes called Forward Agreements.

Futures — Financial derivatives that are traded and cleared on financial exchanges. They allow buyers and sellers of underlying securities to lock in future prices. Futures are fixed commitments to buy or sell specific underlying securities at a future time.

High-Yield Bonds — Corporate bonds with credit ratings below BBB– on the S&P credit rating scale. These bonds typically have higher interest rates than investment grade bonds. They are also known as junk bonds due to their elevated risk.

Indirect Risk — Financial and non-financial risks a company is indirectly exposed to through its vendors or competitors.

In the Money — An option that is in a position to pay out for its owner. An example of an in the money trading position is a call option you own, if the underlying price is above the strike price.

Investment Grade — Corporate bonds with credit ratings at or above BBB– on the S&P credit rating scale. These bonds have high quality and are considered the opposite of junk bonds.

Junk Bonds — Corporate bonds with credit ratings below BBB– on the S&P credit rating scale. These bonds are called junk, because they are of lower credit quality than investment grade bonds. They are also known as high-yield bonds, as they have higher interest rates than investment grade bonds.

Liquidity Risk — Risk that a company will not have enough cash on hand to run its operations.

Market Risk — Financial market risks to a company's operations. These can include commodities, currencies, and interest rates as well as equity and bond market risks.

Operational Risk — Non-financial risk that a company will not be run well. This could relate to management, technology, and other operational areas of a business.

Option Premium — Amount paid to the writer of an option upfront by the buyer of that option. This is the same term for upfront funds paid for calls or puts. The price of options is determined by a number of different factors.

Options — Financial derivatives used to manage financial market risks. There are two kinds of options, puts and calls. These options all are tied to an underlying security, have a fixed duration, an option premium, and a strike price.

Out of the Money — A trading position that is losing. If you have an out of the money trading position, you owe someone money. An example of an out of the money trading position is a call option you have sold/written if the underlying price is below the strike price.

Put — A financial derivatives instrument that derives its value from an underlying security. A put is paid for upfront with an option premium, and it is sold by an option writer. If the price of the underlying security is *below* the strike price, the put is said to be in the money for the buyer of the put option. Puts are often used as hedges against downside price risks, as they pay out to the buyers if prices fall. Puts are the inverse of calls.

Rating Agencies — One of the three major credit rating agencies, including Standard and Poor's (S&P), Moody's, and Fitch. They use rating scales to differentiate corporate bond credit, including a delineation between investment grade and high-yield — or "junk" — bonds.

Regulatory Risk — Risk that laws or regulations could damage a business's ability to operate or be profitable.

Reputation Risk — Risk that a company or business could have its reputation damaged.

Strategic Risk — Risk that a company's strategy is flawed. It may be too far ahead of the market or too far behind competitors.

Strike Price — Price built into an option that determines when a put or a call pays out. Exercised calls pay out if the price of the underlying security is above the strike price. Exercised puts pay out if the price of the underlying security is below the strike price.

Writing an Option — This is another way to say that you sell a call or put option.

ABOUT THE AUTHOR

Jason Schenker is the President of Prestige Economics and the world's top-ranked financial market futurist. Bloomberg News has ranked Mr. Schenker one of the most accurate forecasters in the world in 43 different categories since 2011, including #1 in the world in 25 categories for his forecasts of the Euro, the Pound, the Swiss Franc, the Chinese RMB, crude oil prices, natural gas prices, gold prices, industrial metals prices, agricultural prices, US non-farm payrolls, and US new home sales.

Mr. Schenker has written 11 books and edited two almanacs. Five of his books have been #1 Best Sellers on Amazon, including *Commodity Prices 101*, *Recession-Proof*, *Electing Recession*, *Quantum: Computing Nouveau,* and *Jobs for Robots*. He also edited the #1 Best Seller *The Robot and Automation Almanac - 2018* as well as the 2019 edition of the almanac. Mr. Schenker is also a columnist for *Bloomberg Opinion*. He has appeared as a guest and guest host on Bloomberg Television as well as a guest on CNBC. He is frequently quoted in the press, including *The Wall Street Journal, The New York Times*, and *The Financial Times*.

Prior to founding Prestige Economics, Mr. Schenker worked for McKinsey & Company as a Risk Specialist, where he directed trading and risk initiatives on six continents. Before joining McKinsey, Mr. Schenker worked for Wachovia as an Economist.

Mr. Schenker holds a Master's in Applied Economics from UNC Greensboro, a Master's in Negotiation from CSU Dominguez Hills, a Master's in German from UNC Chapel Hill, and a Bachelor's with distinction in History and German from The University of Virginia. He also holds a certificate in FinTech from MIT, an executive certificate in Supply Chain Management from MIT, a graduate certificate in Professional Development from UNC, a certificate in Negotiation from Harvard Law School, and a certificate in Cybersecurity from Carnegie Mellon University.

Mr. Schenker holds the professional designations ERP® (Energy Risk Professional), CMT® (Chartered Market Technician), CVA® (Certified Valuation Analyst), CFP® (Certified Financial Planner), and FLTA™ (Certified Futurist and Long-Term Analyst). Mr. Schenker is also an instructor for LinkedIn Learning. His courses include topics about financial risk management, economic indicators, recession-proof strategies, and audit and due diligence.

Mr. Schenker is a member of the Texas Business Leadership Council, the only CEO-based public policy research organization in Texas, with a limited membership of 100 CEOs and Presidents. He is also a member of the 2018 Director class of the Texas Lyceum, a non-partisan, nonprofit that fosters business and policy dialogue on important US and Texas issues.

Mr. Schenker is an active executive in FinTech as a member of the Central Texas Angel Network and as the Executive Director of the Texas Blockchain Association. He is also a member of the National Association of Corporate Directors as well as an NACD Board Governance Fellow.

In October 2016, Mr. Schenker founded The Futurist Institute to help analysts, strategists, and economists become futurists through a training and certification program. Participants can earn the FLTA — Certified Futurist and Long-Term Analyst designation.

Mr. Schenker was ranked one of the top 100 most influential financial advisors in the world by Investopedia in June 2018.

For more information about Jason Schenker:
www.jasonschenker.com

For more information about The Futurist Institute:
www.futuristinstitute.org

For more information about Prestige Economics:
www.prestigeeconomics.com

TOP FORECASTER ACCURACY RANKINGS

Prestige Economics has been recognized as the most accurate independent commodity and financial market research firm in the world. As the only forecaster for Prestige Economics, Jason Schenker is very proud that Bloomberg News has ranked him a top forecaster in 43 different categories since 2011, including #1 in the world in 25 different forecast categories.

Mr. Schenker has been top ranked as a forecaster of economic indicators, energy prices, metals prices, agricultural prices, and foreign exchange rates.

ECONOMIC TOP RANKINGS

#1 Non-Farm Payroll Forecaster in the World
#1 New Home Sales Forecaster in the World
#2 US Unemployment Rate Forecaster in the World
#3 Durable Goods Orders Forecaster in the World
#6 Consumer Confidence Forecaster in the World
#7 ISM Manufacturing Index Forecaster in the World
#7 US Housing Start Forecaster in the World

ENERGY PRICE TOP RANKINGS

#1 WTI Crude Oil Price Forecaster in the World

#1 Brent Crude Oil Price Forecaster in the World

#1 Henry Hub Natural Gas Price Forecaster in the World

METALS PRICE TOP RANKINGS

#1 Gold Price Forecaster in the World

#1 Platinum Price Forecaster in the World

#1 Palladium Price Forecaster in the World

#1 Industrial Metals Price Forecaster in the World

#1 Copper Price Forecaster in the World

#1 Aluminum Price Forecaster in the World

#1 Nickel Price Forecaster in the World

#1 Tin Price Forecaster in the World

#1 Zinc Price Forecaster in the World

#2 Precious Metals Price Forecaster in the World

#2 Silver Price Forecaster in the World

#2 Lead Price Forecaster in the World

#2 Iron Ore Forecaster in the World

AGRICULTURAL PRICE TOP RANKINGS

#1 Coffee Price Forecaster in the World

#1 Cotton Price Forecaster in the World

#1 Sugar Price Forecaster in the World

#1 Soybean Price Forecaster in the World

FOREIGN EXCHANGE TOP RANKINGS

#1 Euro Forecaster in the World

#1 British Pound Forecaster in the World

#1 Swiss Franc Forecaster in the World

#1 Chinese RMB Forecaster in the World

#1 Russian Ruble Forecaster in the World

#1 Brazilian Real Forecaster in the World

#2 Turkish Lira Forecaster in the World

#3 Major Currency Forecaster in the World

#3 Canadian Dollar Forecaster in the World

#4 Japanese Yen Forecaster in the World

#5 Australian Dollar Forecaster in the World

#7 Mexican Peso Forecaster in the World

#1 EURCHF Forecaster in the World

#2 EURJPY Forecaster in the World

#2 EURGBP Forecaster in the World

#2 EURRUB Forecaster in the World

ABOUT THE PUBLISHER

Prestige Professional Publishing LLC was founded in 2011 to produce insightful and timely professional reference books. We are registered with the Library of Congress.

Published Titles

Be the Shredder, Not the Shred

Commodity Prices 101

Electing Recession

Financial Risk Management Fundamentals

A Gentle Introduction to Audit and Due Diligence

Jobs for Robots

Midterm Economics

The Promise of Blockchain

Quantum: Computing Nouveau

Robot-Proof Yourself

The Robot and Automation Almanac — 2018

The Robot and Automation Almanac — 2019

Future Titles

The Fog of Data

Futureproof Supply Chain

Spikes: Growth Hacking Leadership

THE ROBOT AND AUTOMATION ALMANAC

The Robot and Automation Almanac: 2019 is a collection of essays by robot and automation experts, executives, and investors on the big trends to watch for in automation, AI, and robotics in 2019. *The Robot and Automation Almanac: 2019* was compiled by The Futurist Institute and published by Prestige Professional Publishing in December 2018.

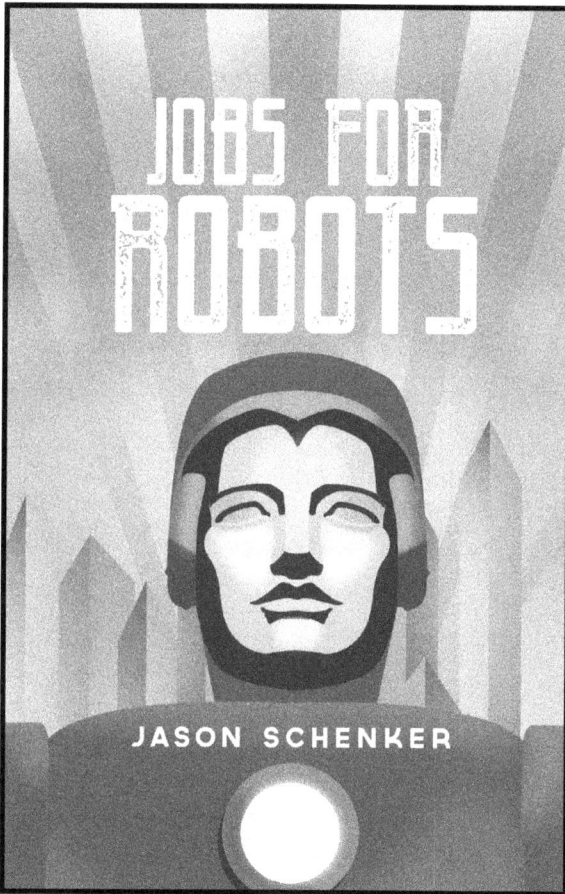

Jobs for Robots provides an in-depth look at the future of automation and robots, with a focus on the opportunities as well as the risks ahead. Job creation in coming years will be extremely strong for the kind of workers that do not require payroll taxes, health care, or vacation: robots. *Jobs for Robots* was published in February 2017. This book has been a #1 Best Seller on Amazon.

ROBOT-PROOF YOURSELF

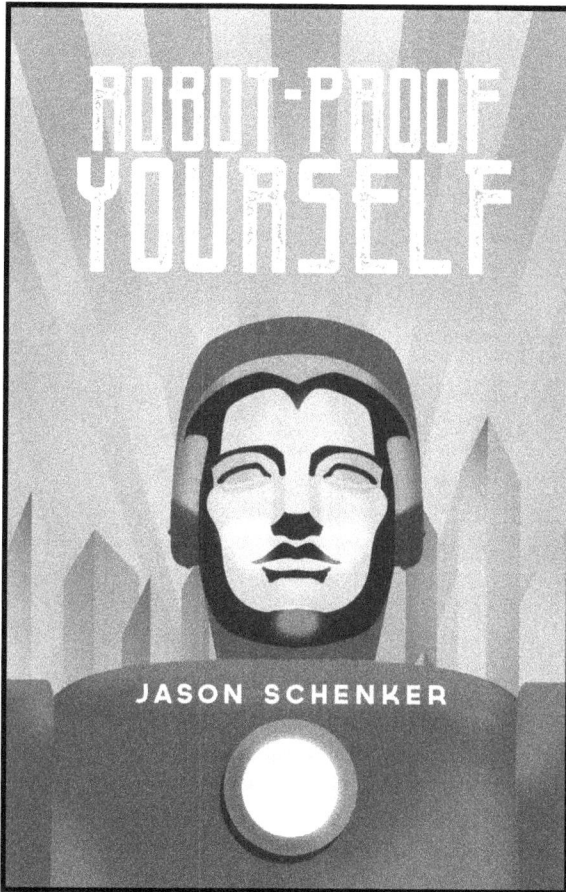

Robot-Proof Yourself offers a number of practical professional recommendations for how to be robot-proof in the coming era of professional, economic, and financial disruptions. Robots and automation are set to advance, but individuals have a chance to benefit from the coming changes. *Robot-Proof Yourself* was released in December 2017.

Spikes: Growth Hacking Leadership presents proactive strategies to help individuals advance rapidly in their professional careers by hacking the system. This book is slated to be published in early 2019 by Prestige Professional Publishing.

DISCLAIMER

FROM THE AUTHOR

The following disclaimer applies to any content in this book:

This book is commentary intended for general information use only and is not investment advice. Jason Schenker does not make recommendations on any specific or general investments, investment types, asset classes, non-regulated markets, specific equities, bonds, or other investment vehicles. Jason Schenker does not guarantee the completeness or accuracy of analyses and statements in this book, nor does Jason Schenker assume any liability for any losses that may result from the reliance by any person or entity on this information. Opinions, forecasts, and information are subject to change without notice. This book does not represent a solicitation or offer of financial or advisory services or products; this book is only market commentary intended and written for general information use only. This book does not constitute investment advice. All links were correct and active at the time this book was published.

DISCLAIMER

FROM THE PUBLISHER

The following disclaimer applies to any content in this book:

This book is commentary intended for general information use only and is not investment advice. Prestige Professional Publishing LLC does not make recommendations on any specific or general investments, investment types, asset classes, non-regulated markets, specific equities, bonds, or other investment vehicles. Prestige Professional Publishing LLC does not guarantee the completeness or accuracy of analyses and statements in this book, nor does Prestige Professional Publishing LLC assume any liability for any losses that may result from the reliance by any person or entity on this information. Opinions, forecasts, and information are subject to change without notice. This book does not represent a solicitation or offer of financial or advisory services or products; this book is only market commentary intended and written for general information use only. This book does not constitute investment advice. All links were correct and active at the time this book was published.

Prestige Professional Publishing LLC

7101 Fig Vine Cove

Austin, Texas 78750

www.prestigeprofessionalpublishing.com

ISBN: 978-1-946197-25-2 *Paperback*
   978-1-946197-19-1 *Ebook*

www.ingramcontent.com/pod-product-compliance
Lightning Source LLC
Chambersburg PA
CBHW061253220326
41599CB00028B/5630